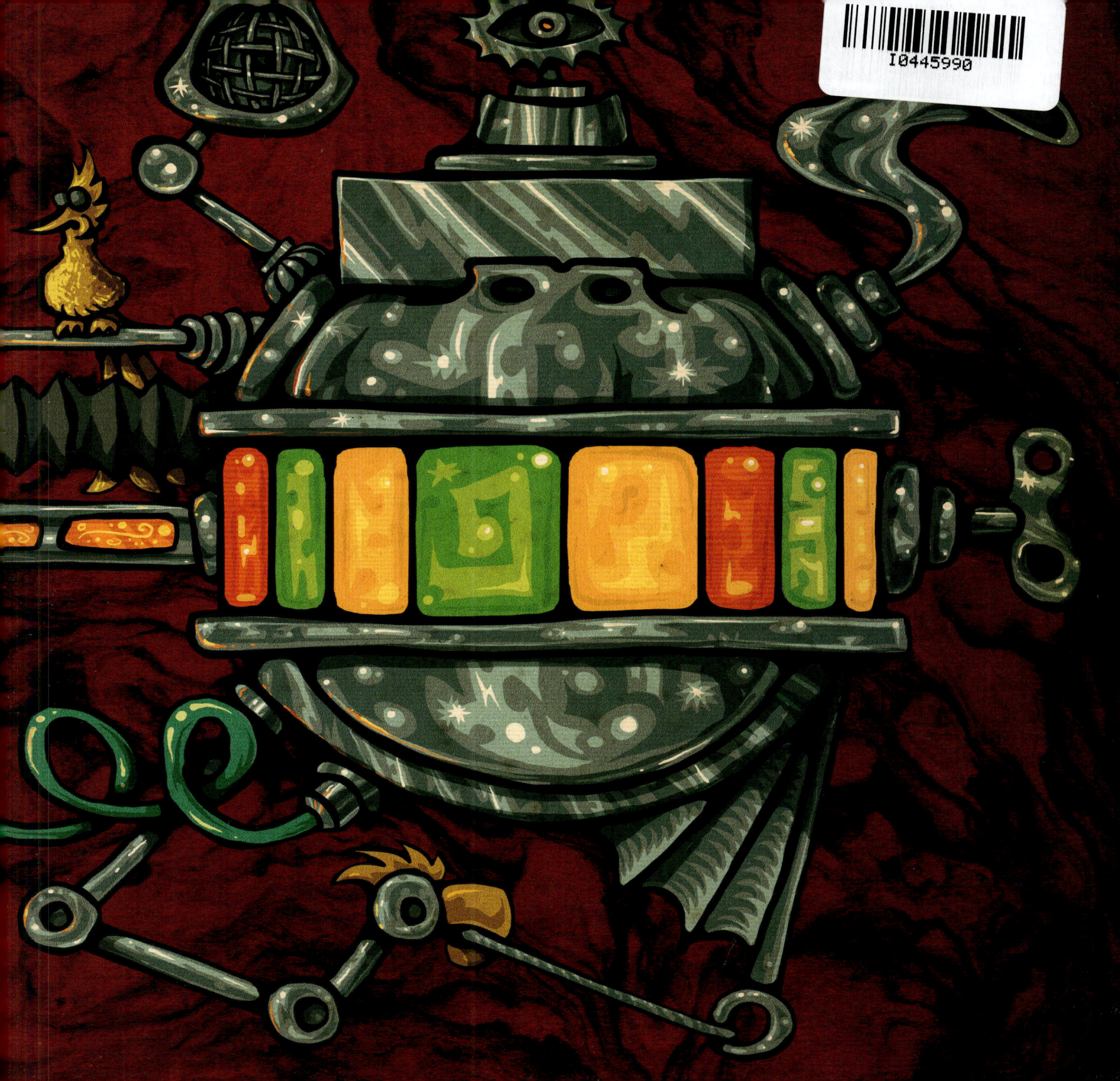

For my mad trio M, W 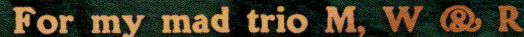 & R

First published by Velocity Press 2024

velocitypress.uk
jempanufnik.com

Printed and bound in China by
Everbest Printing Co Ltd.

ISBN: 9781913231590

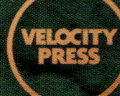

Jem Stone's
LEGEND OF
KAPTAIN KARNIVAL

Music & pictures by
JEM PANUFNIK

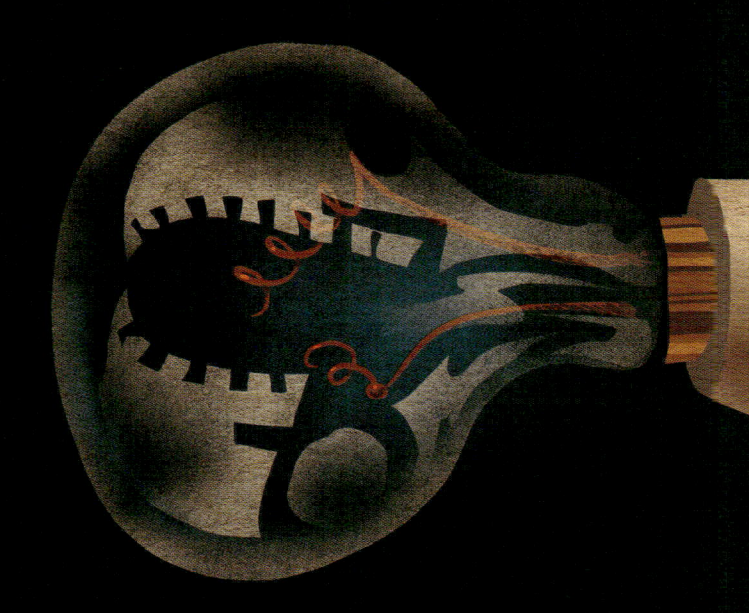

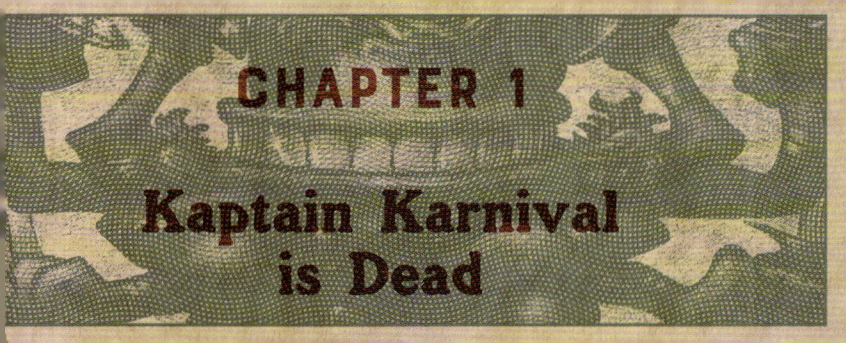

CHAPTER 1

Kaptain Karnival
is Dead

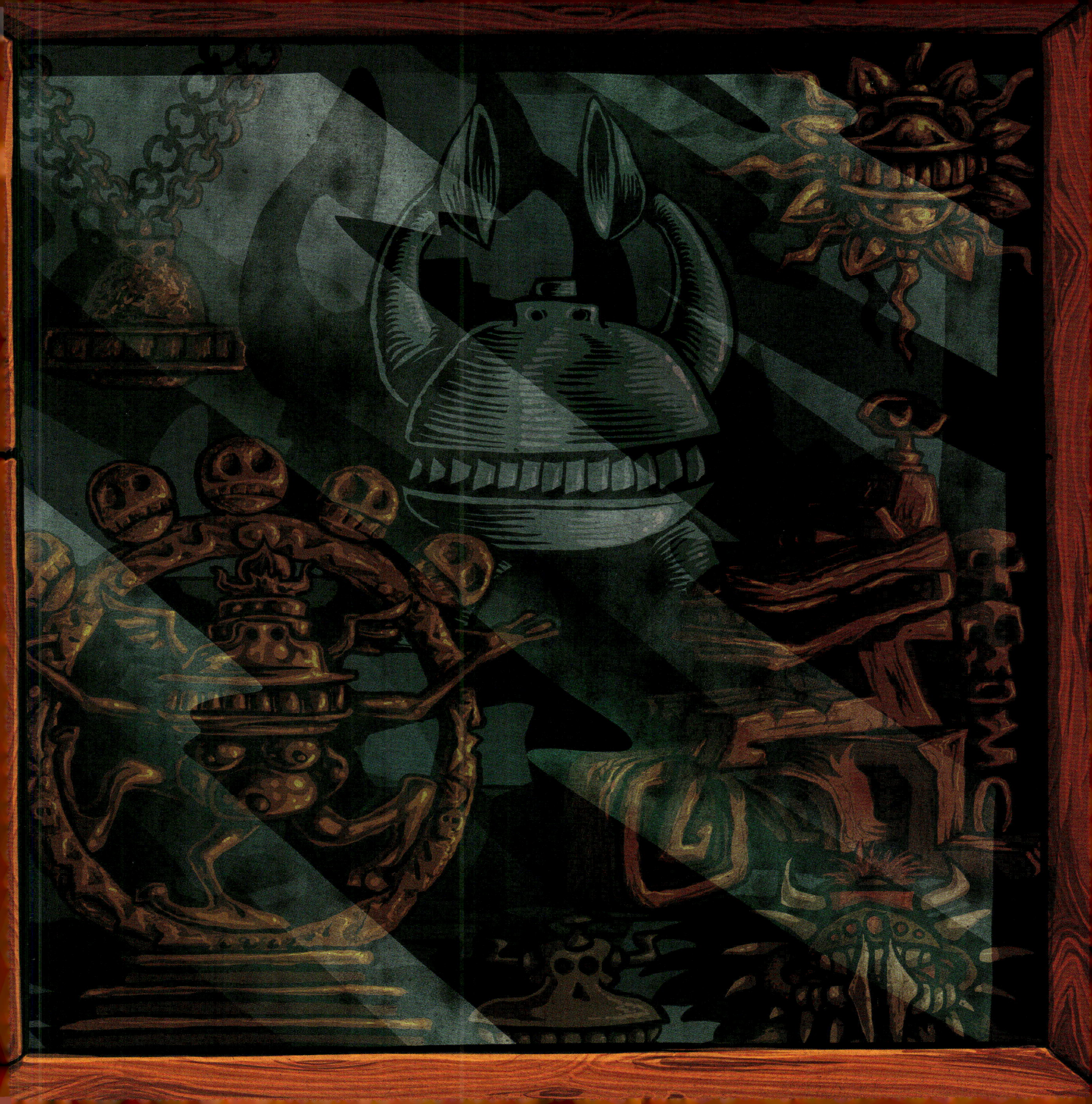

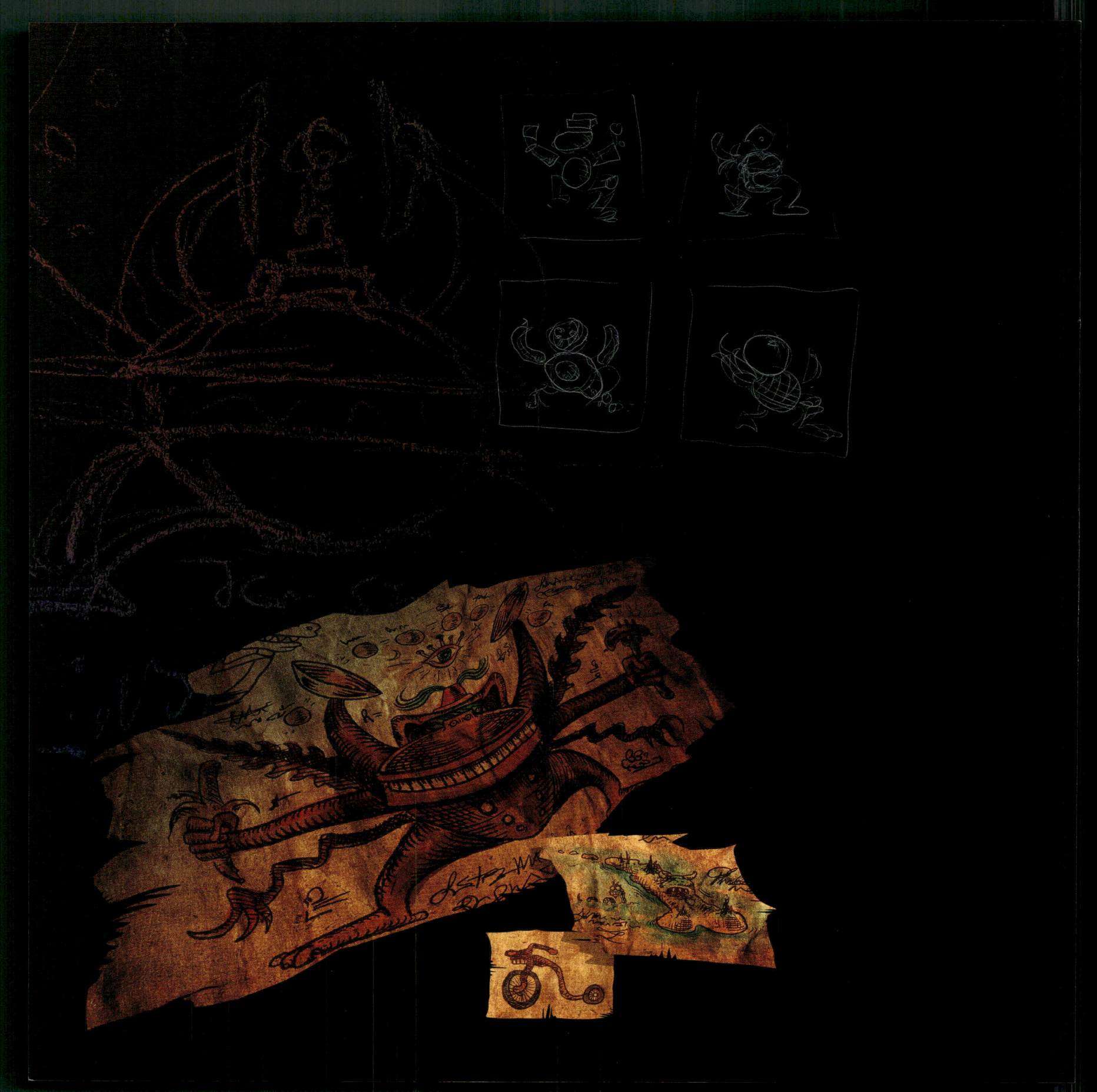

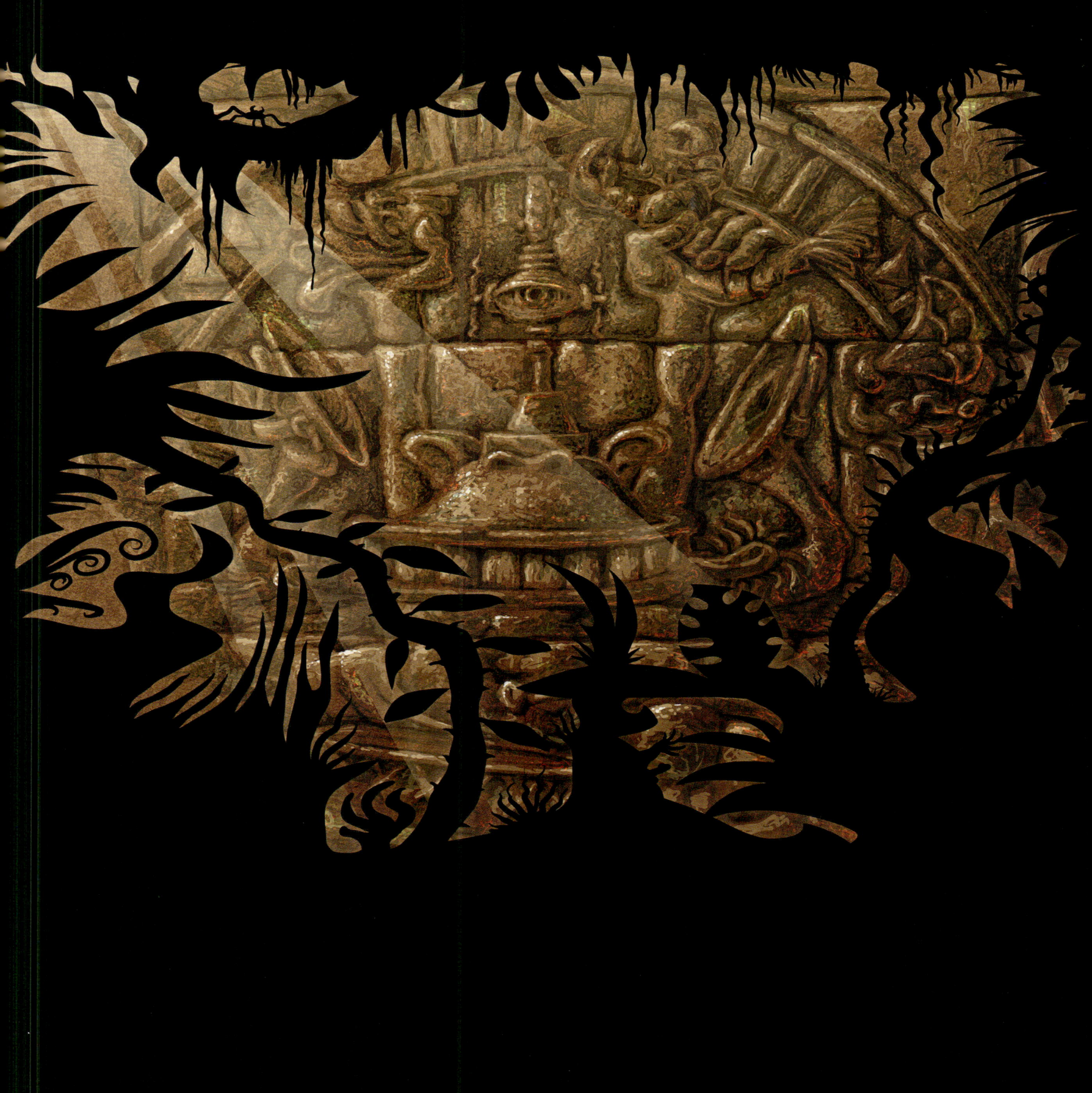

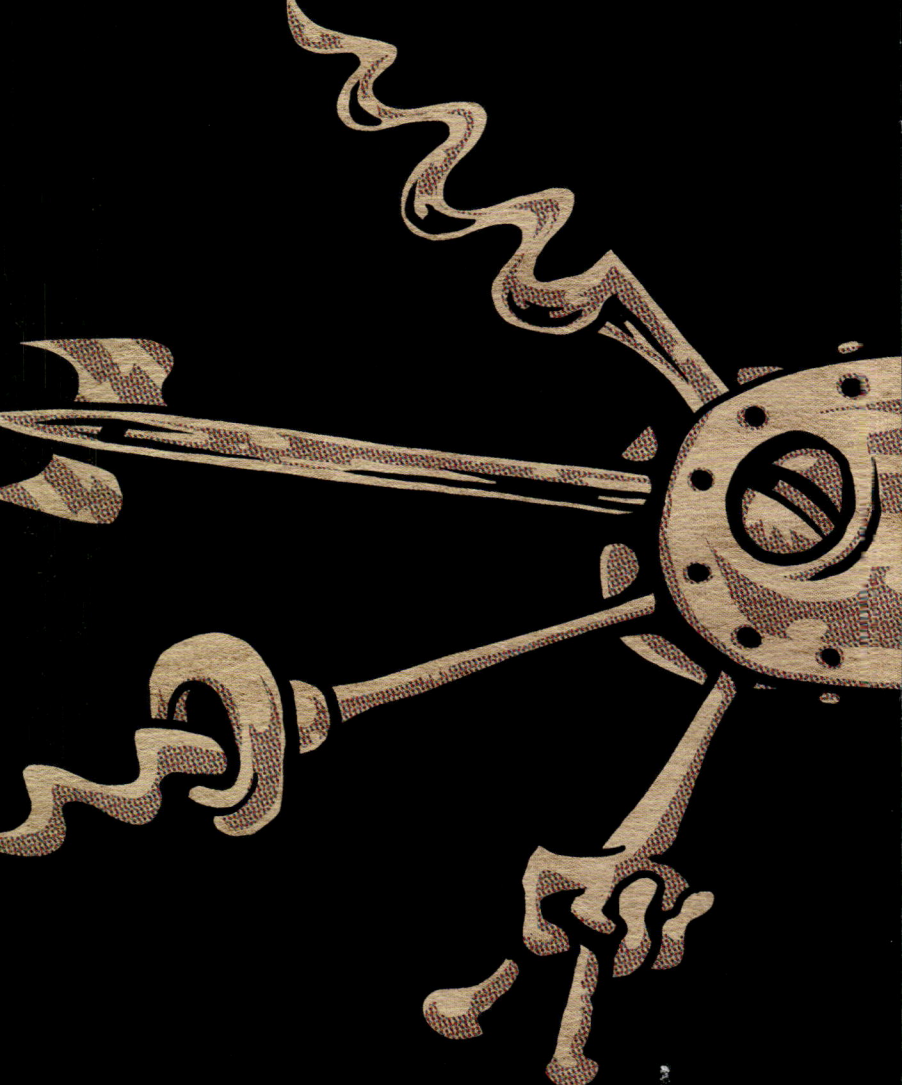

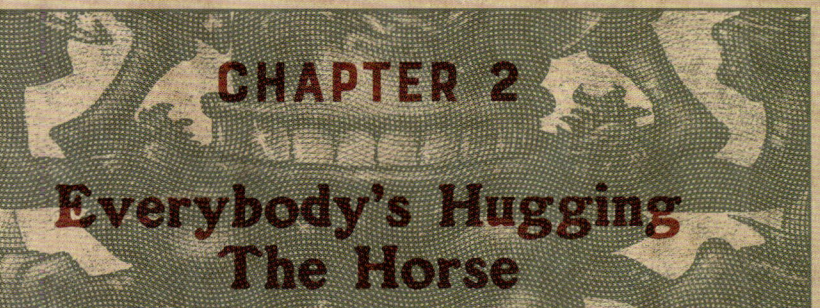

CHAPTER 2

Everybody's Hugging The Horse

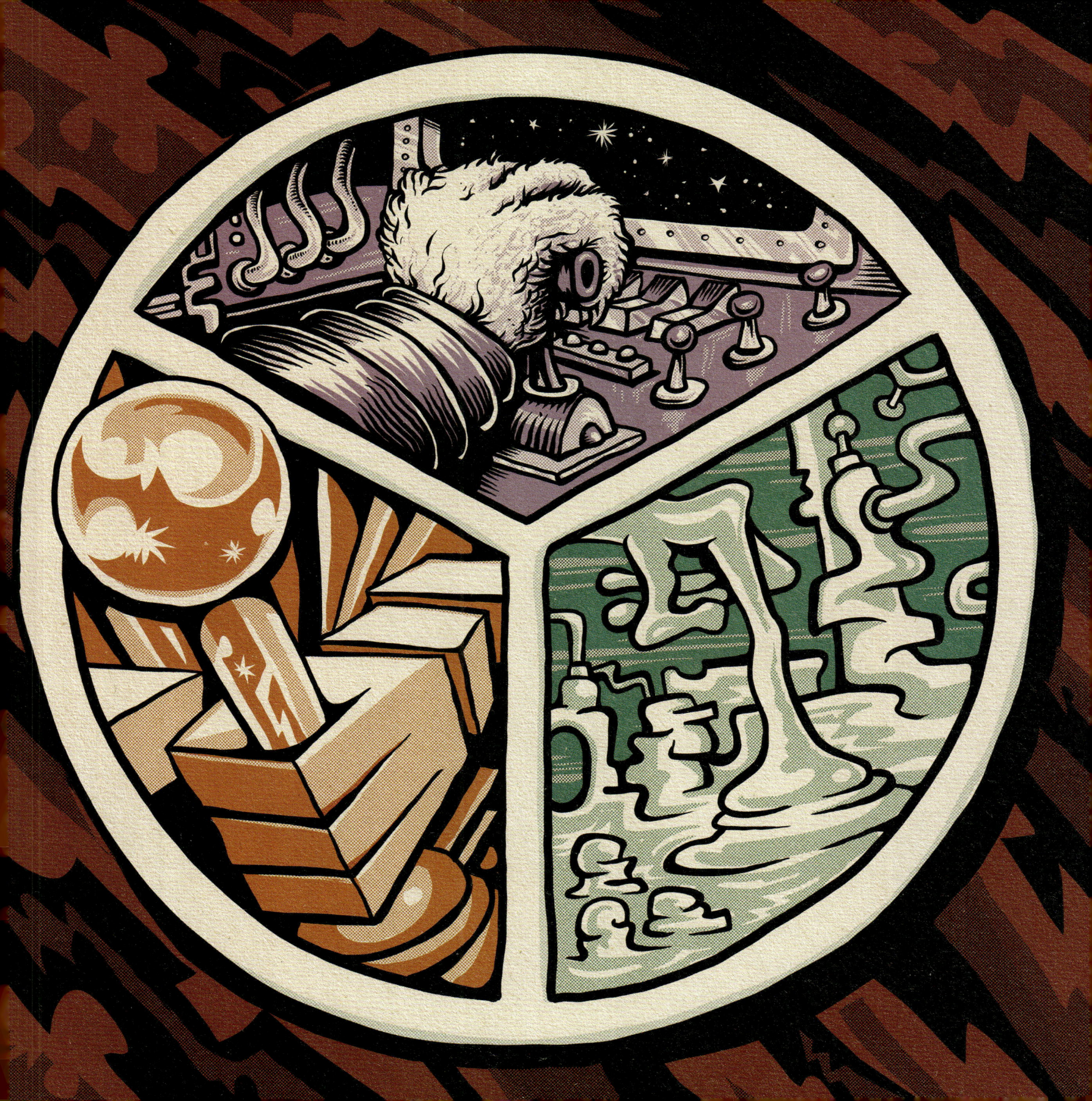

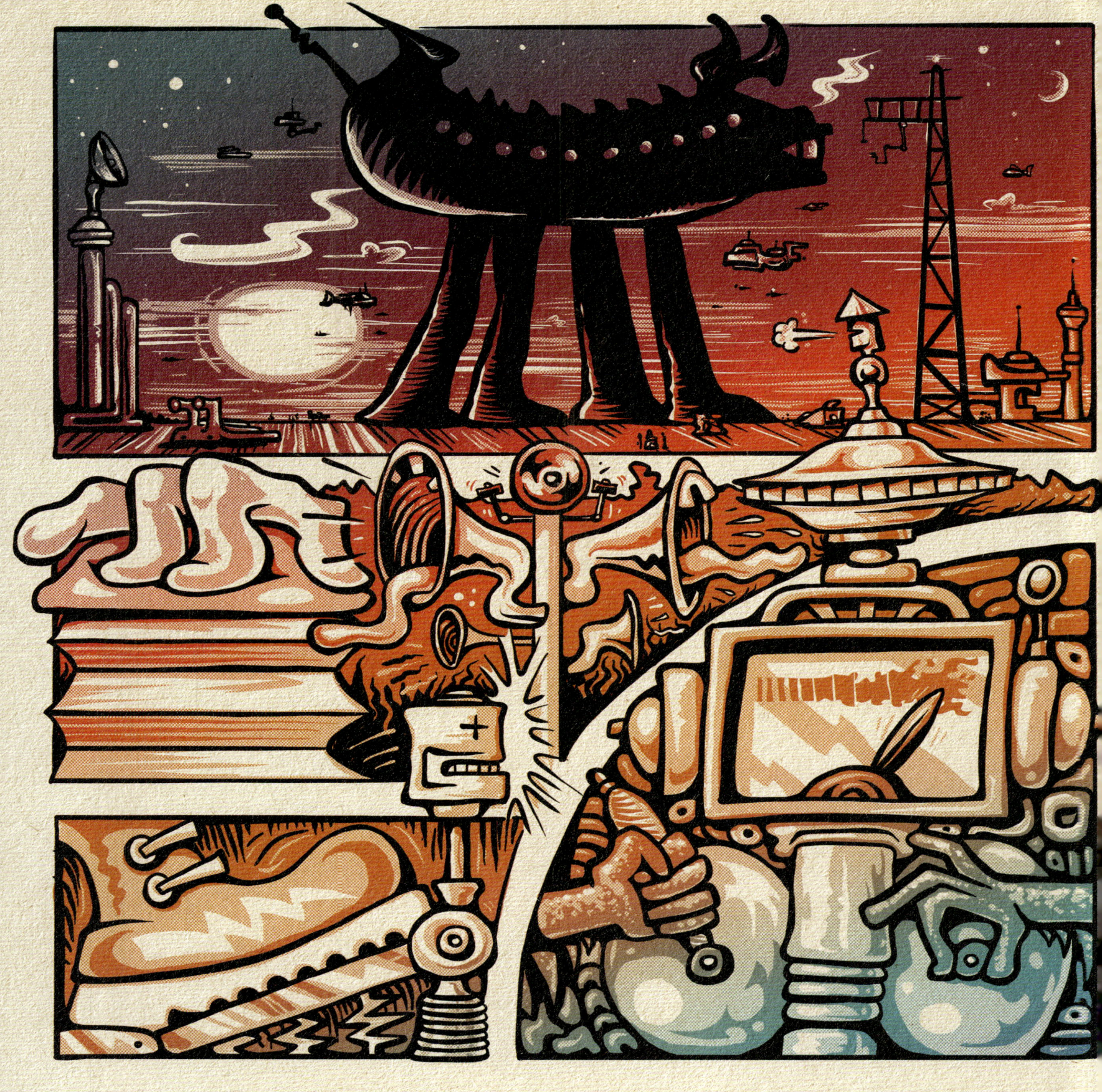

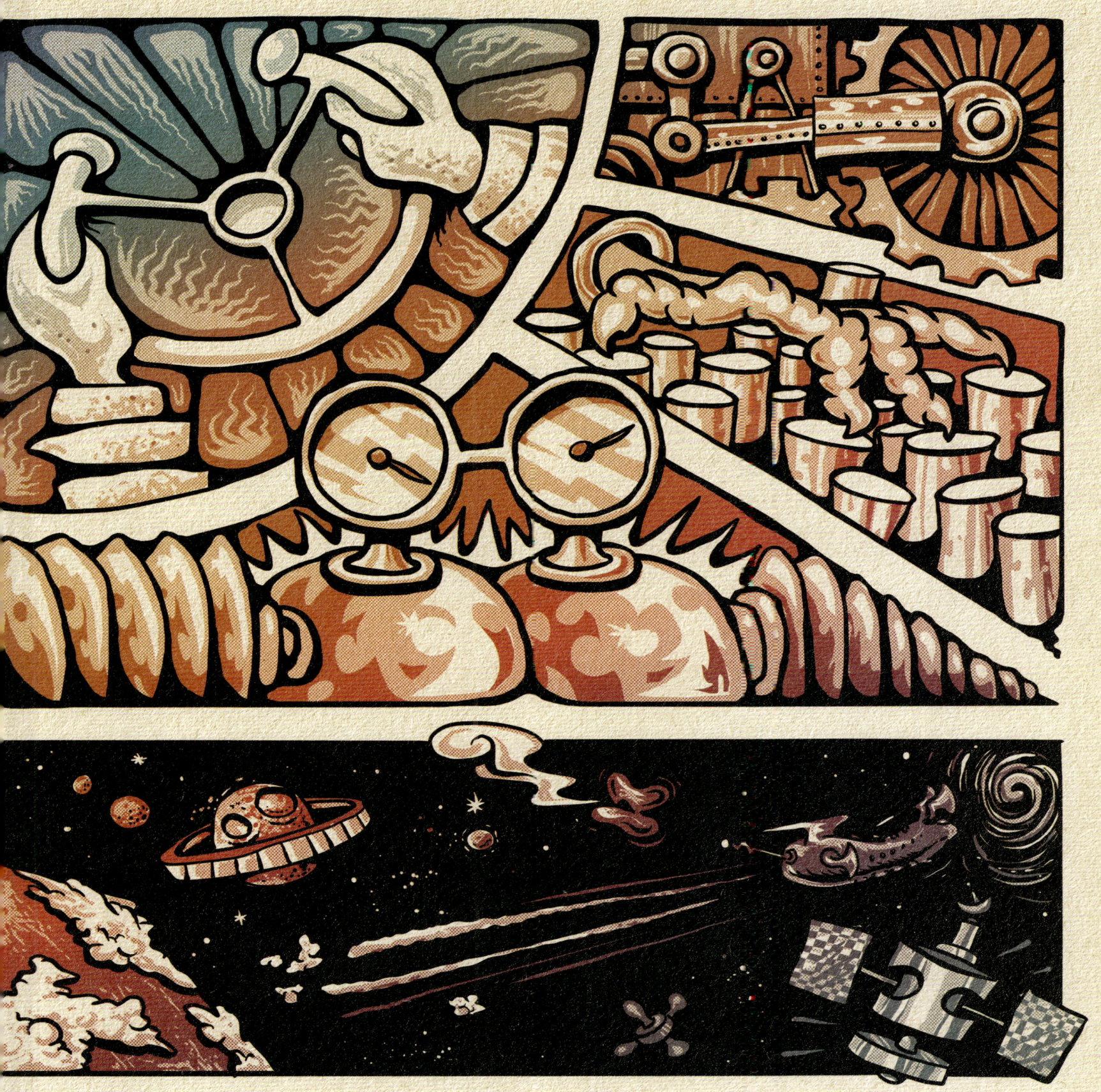

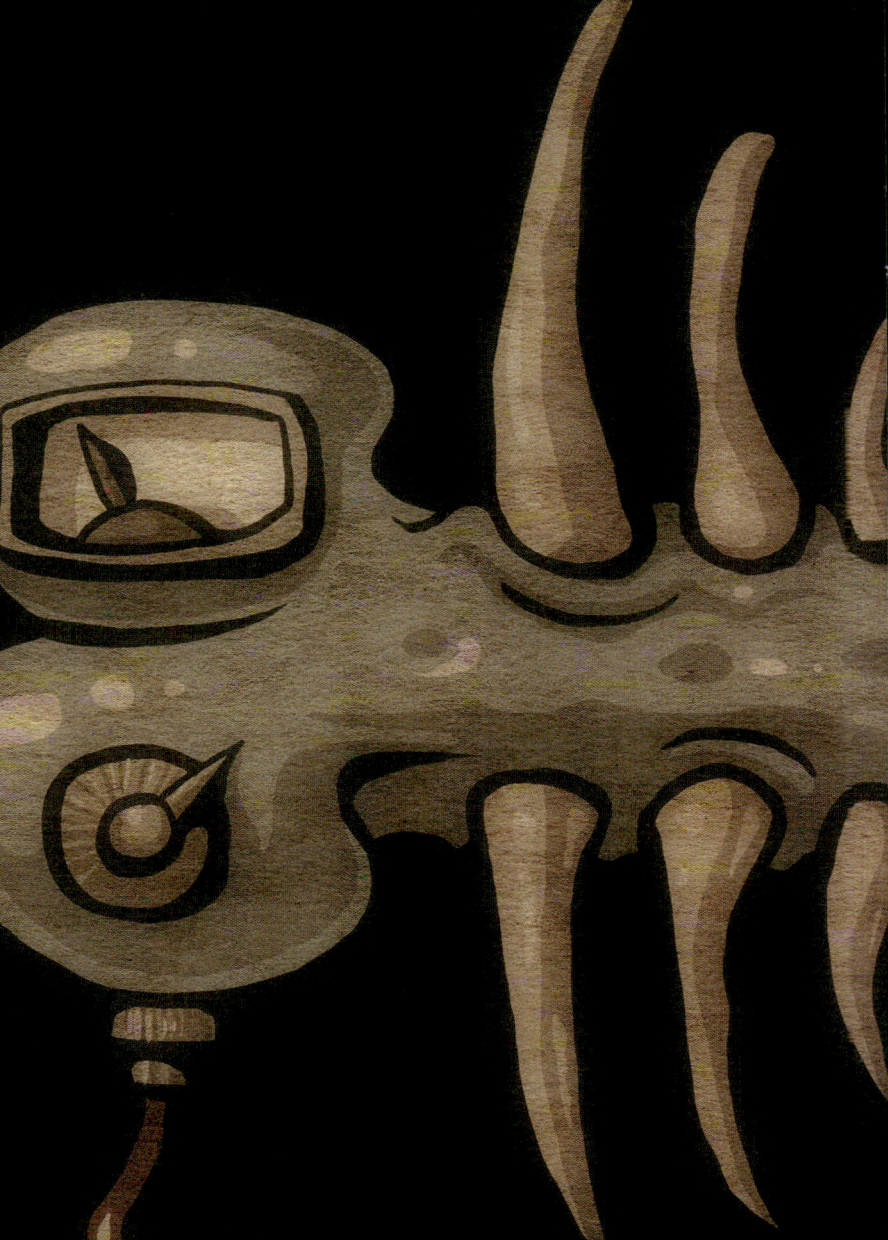

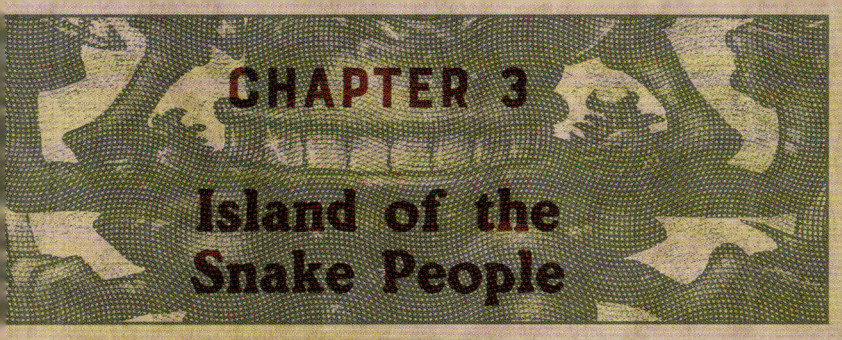

CHAPTER 3

Island of the Snake People

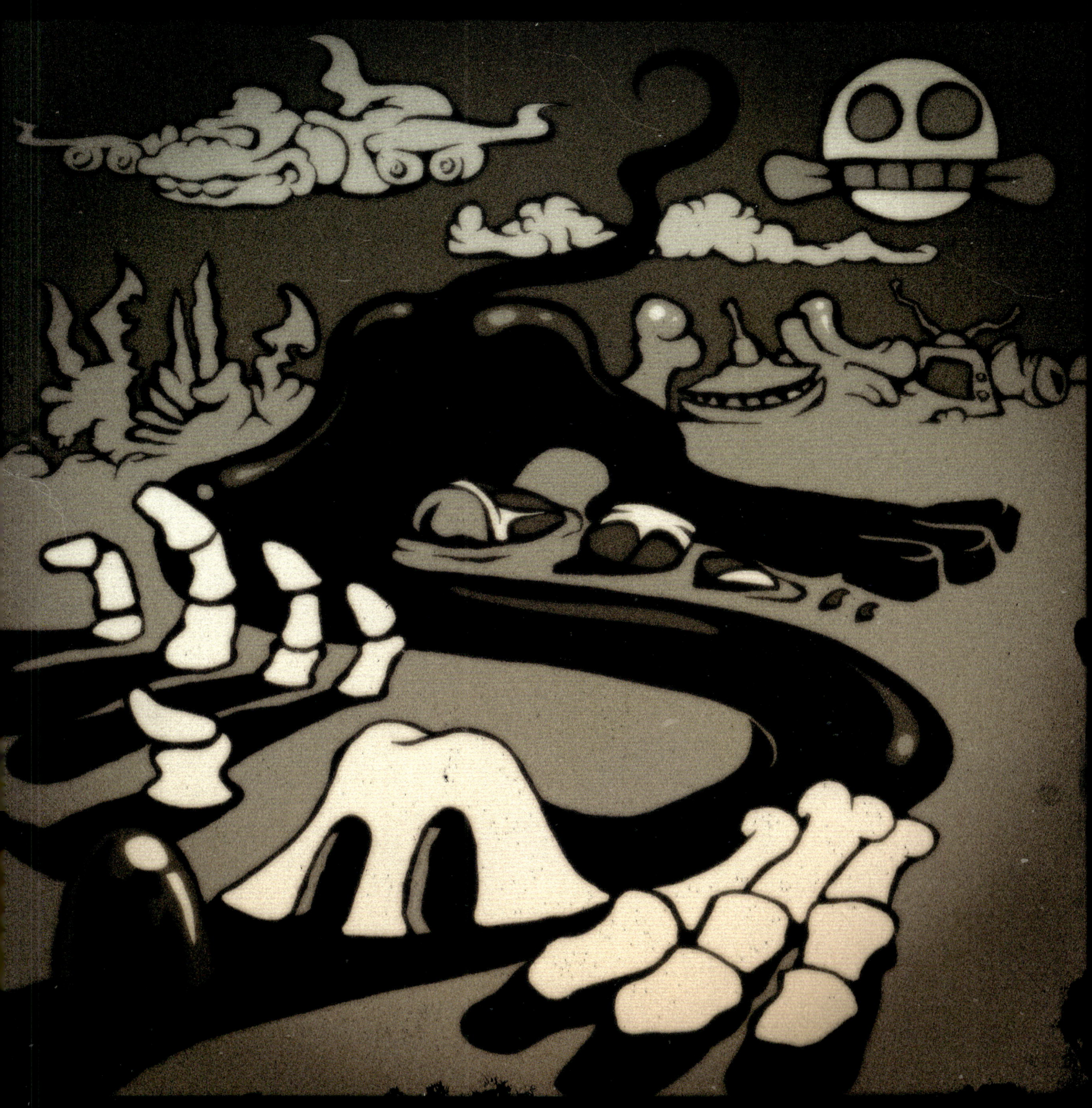

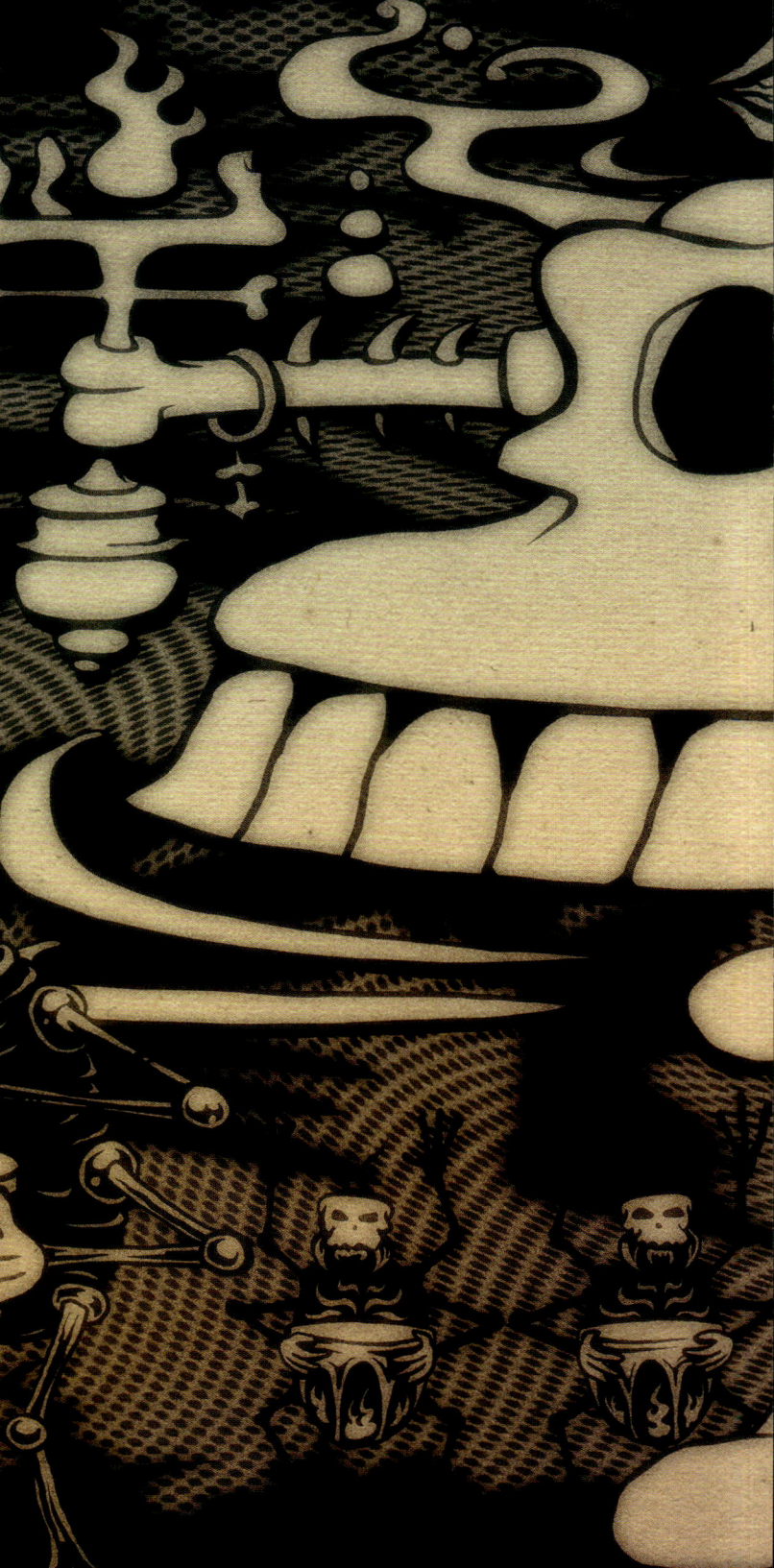

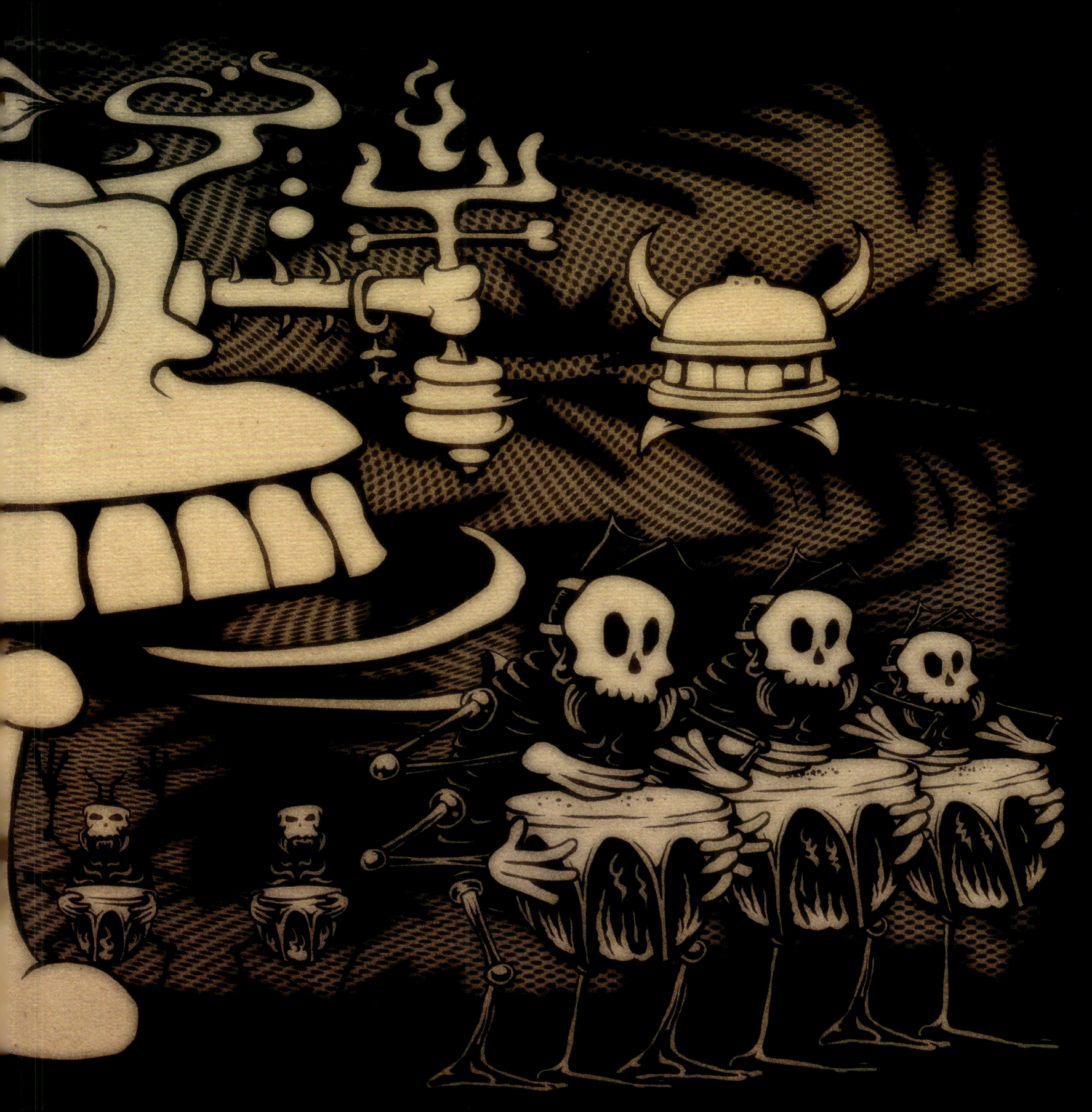

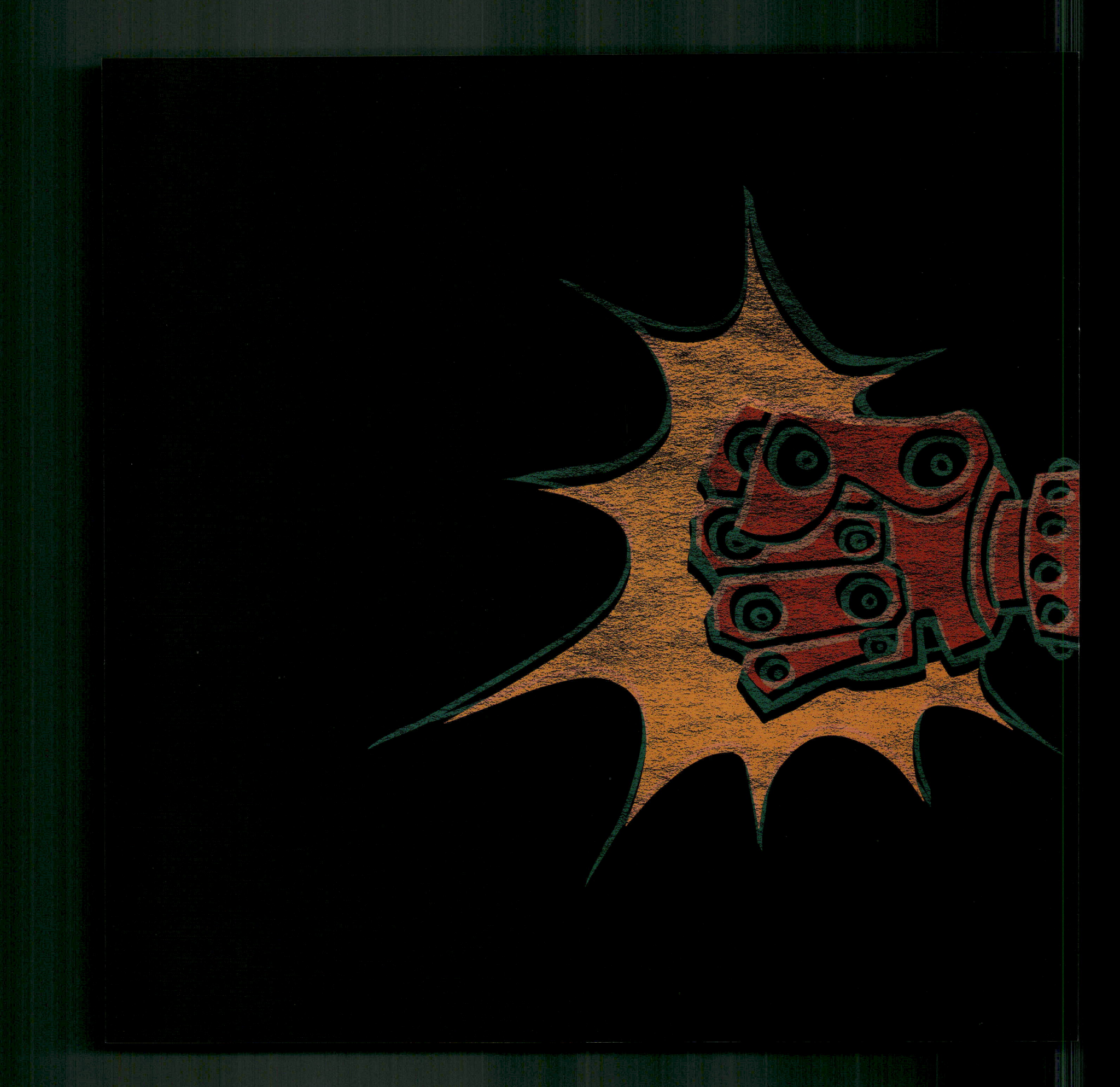

CHAPTER 4

Cardiac Cadillac

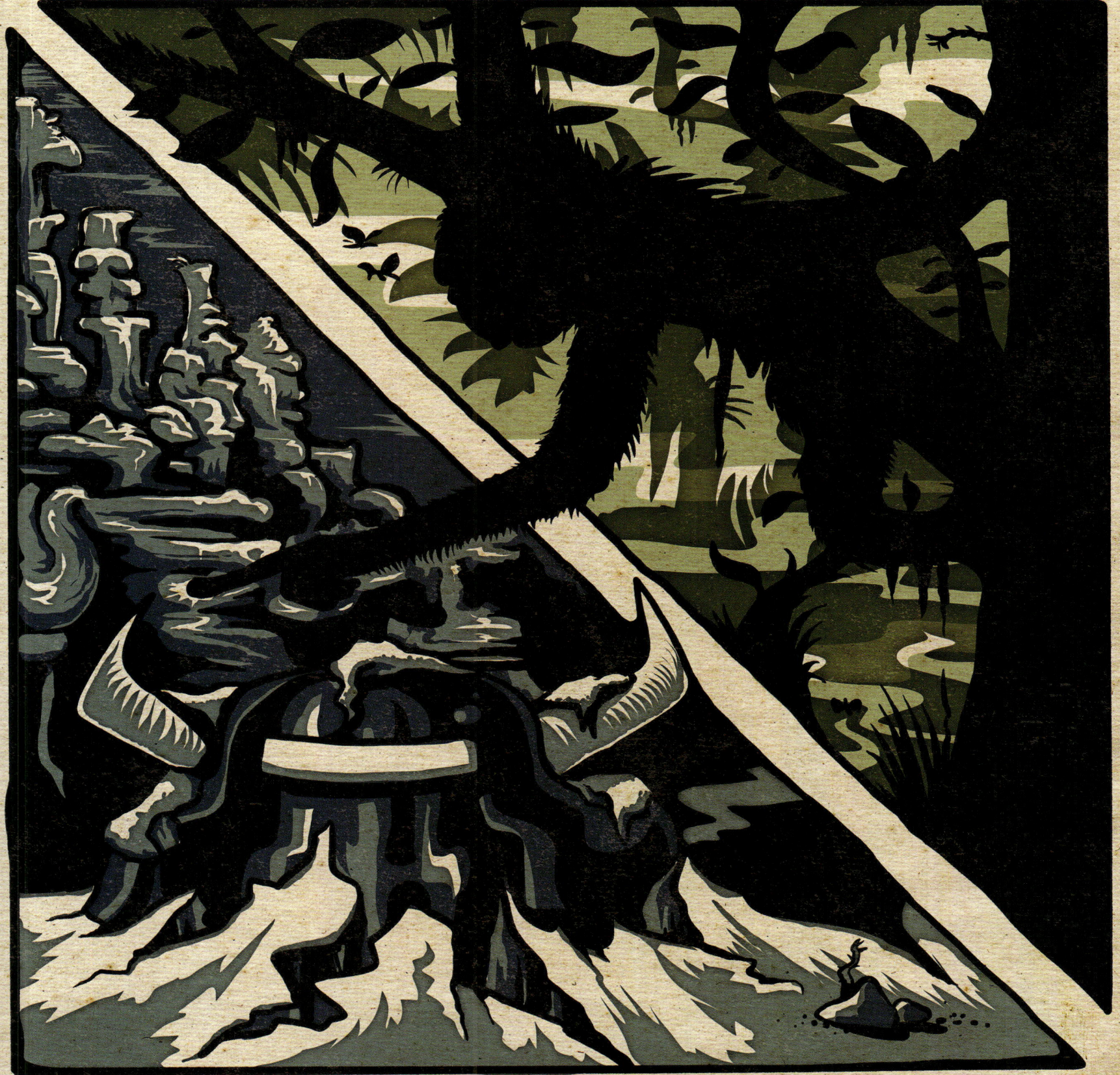

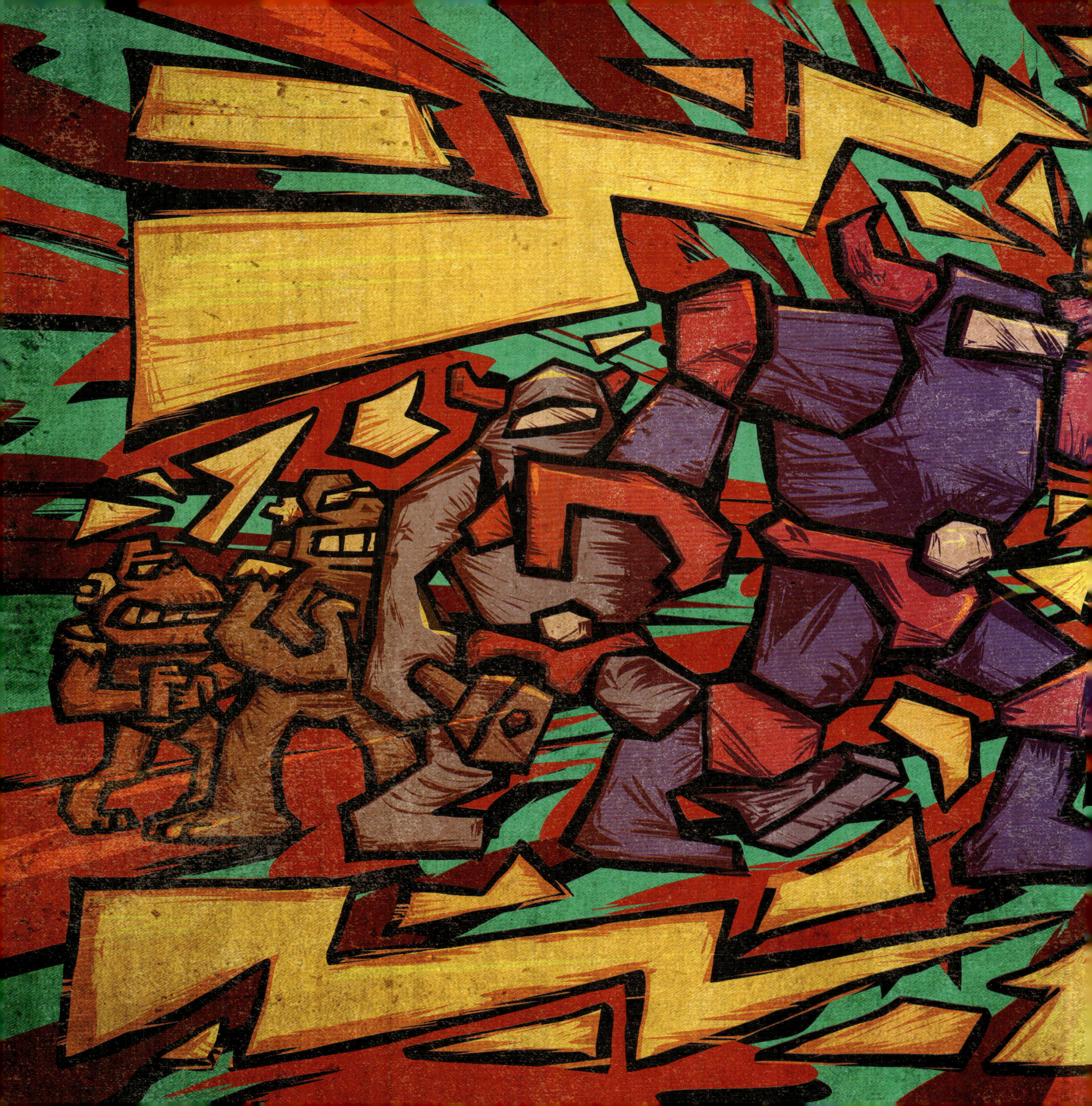

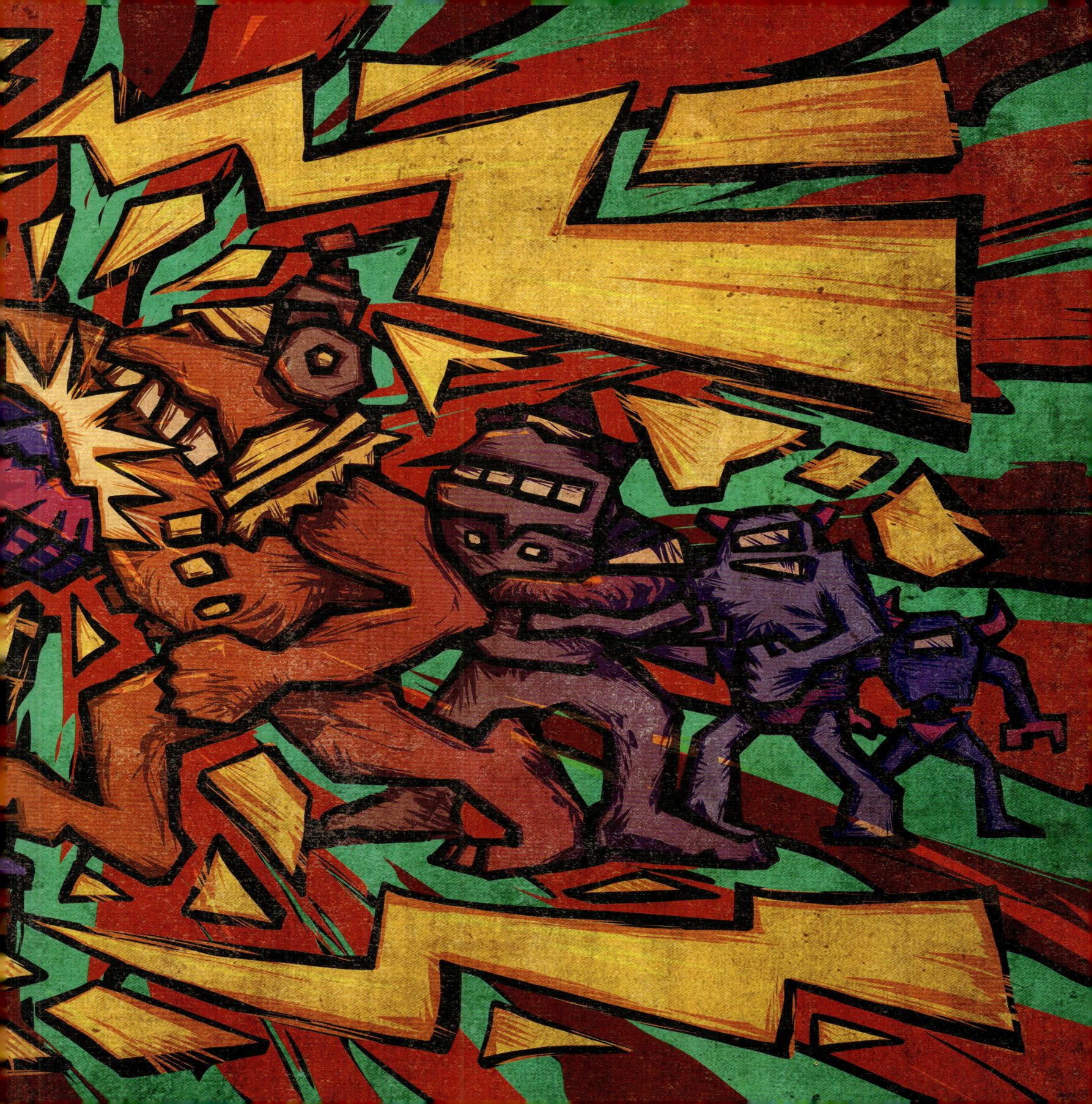

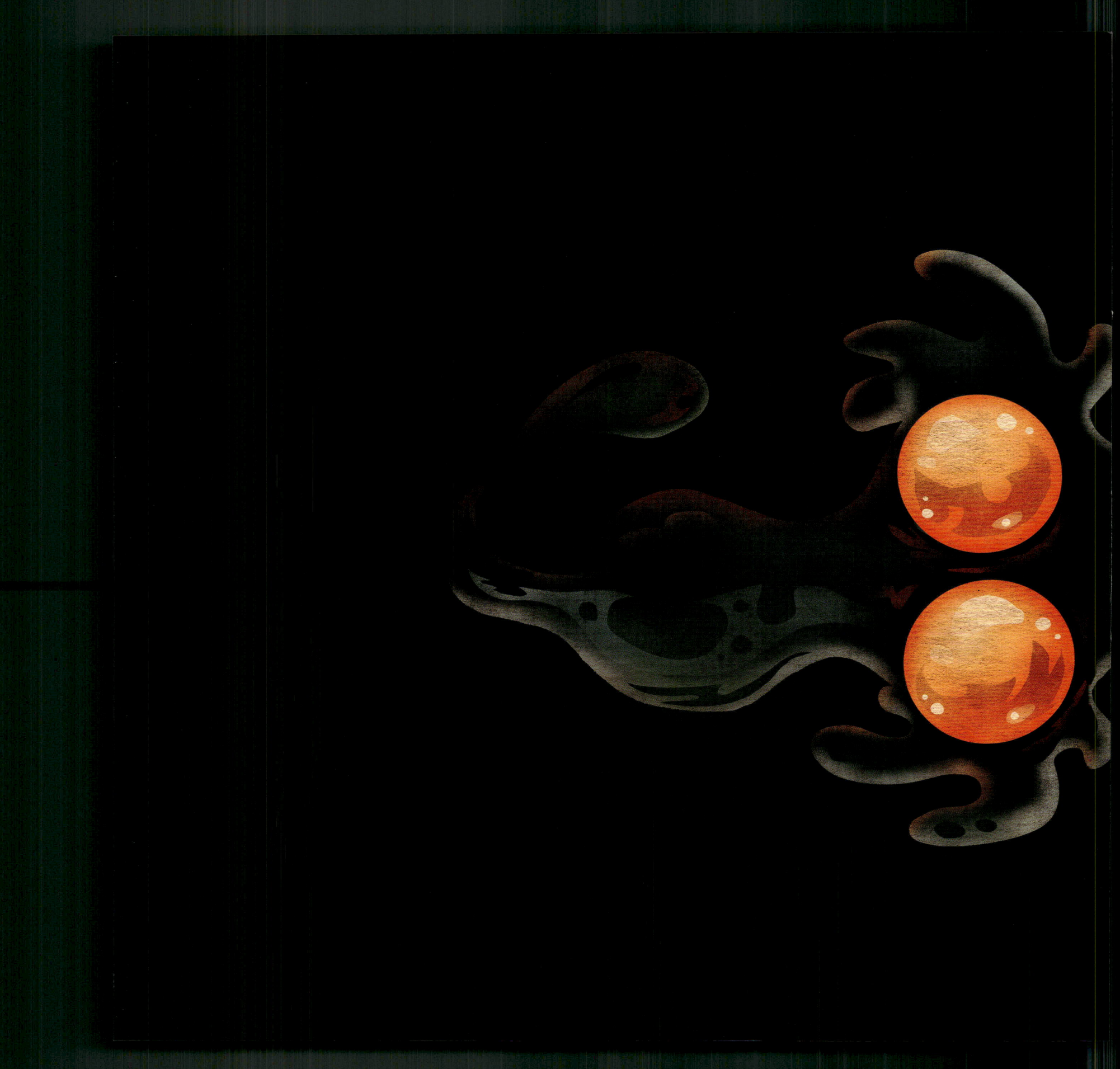

CHAPTER 5

Voluptuoso

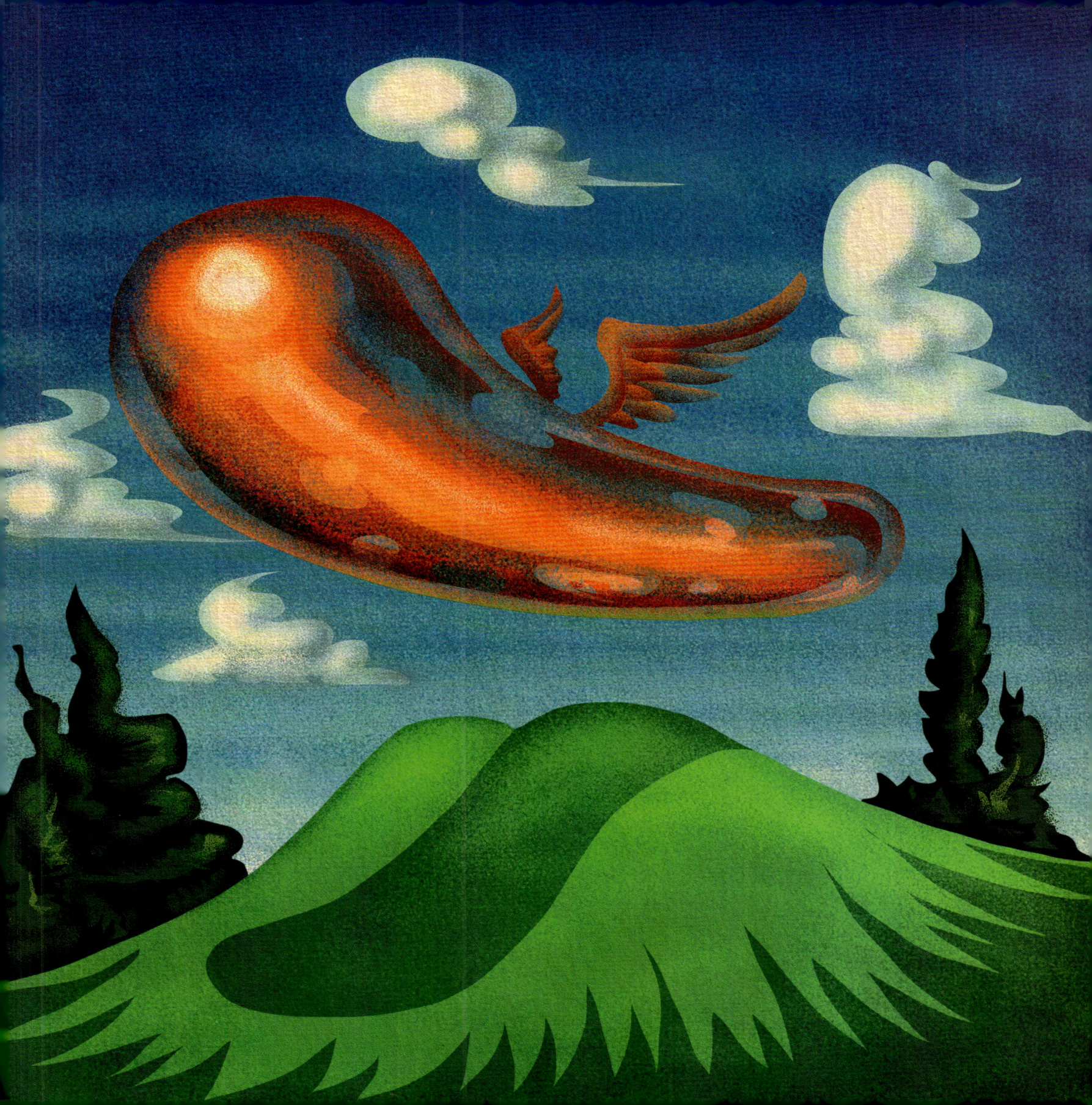

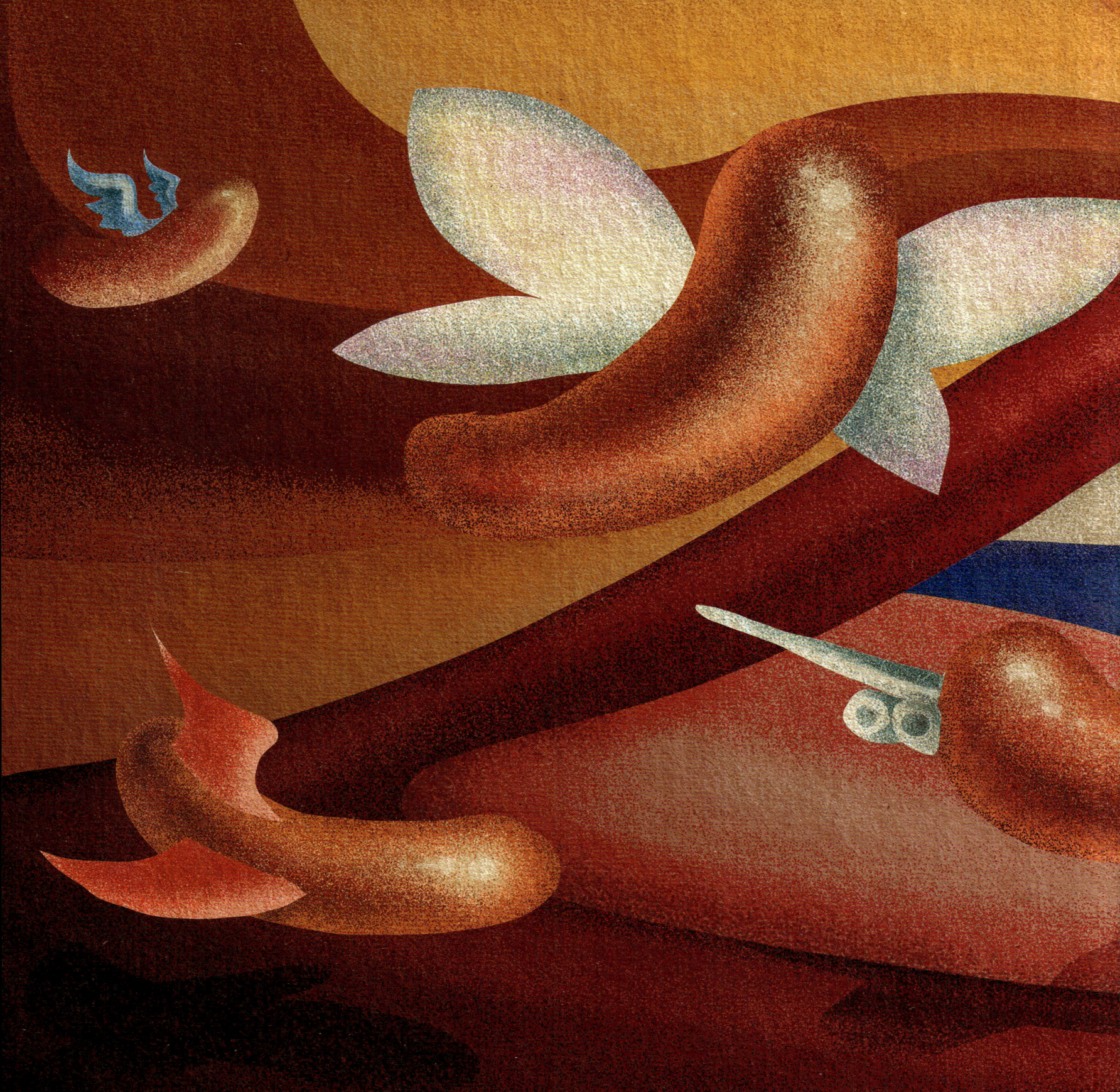

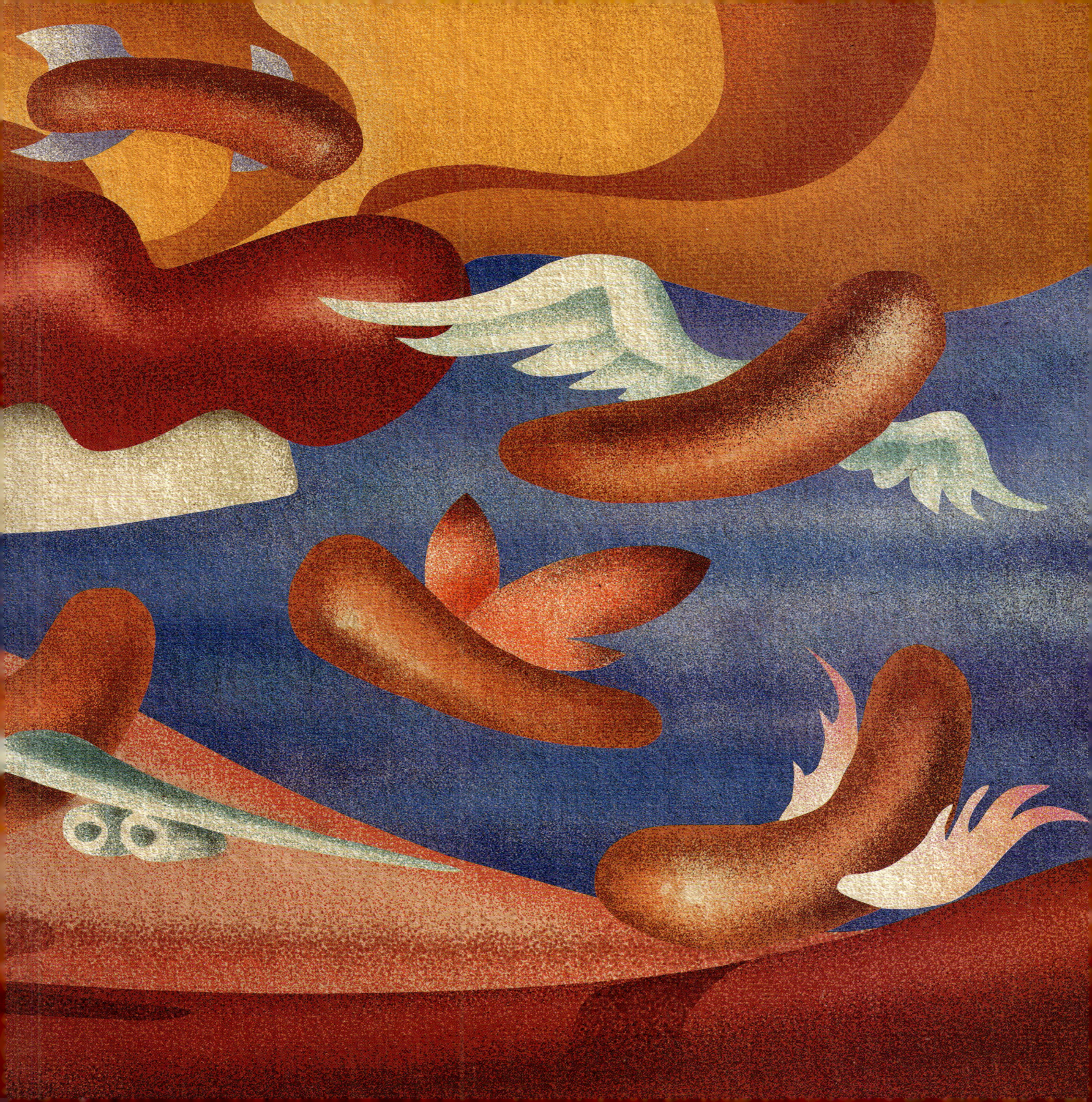

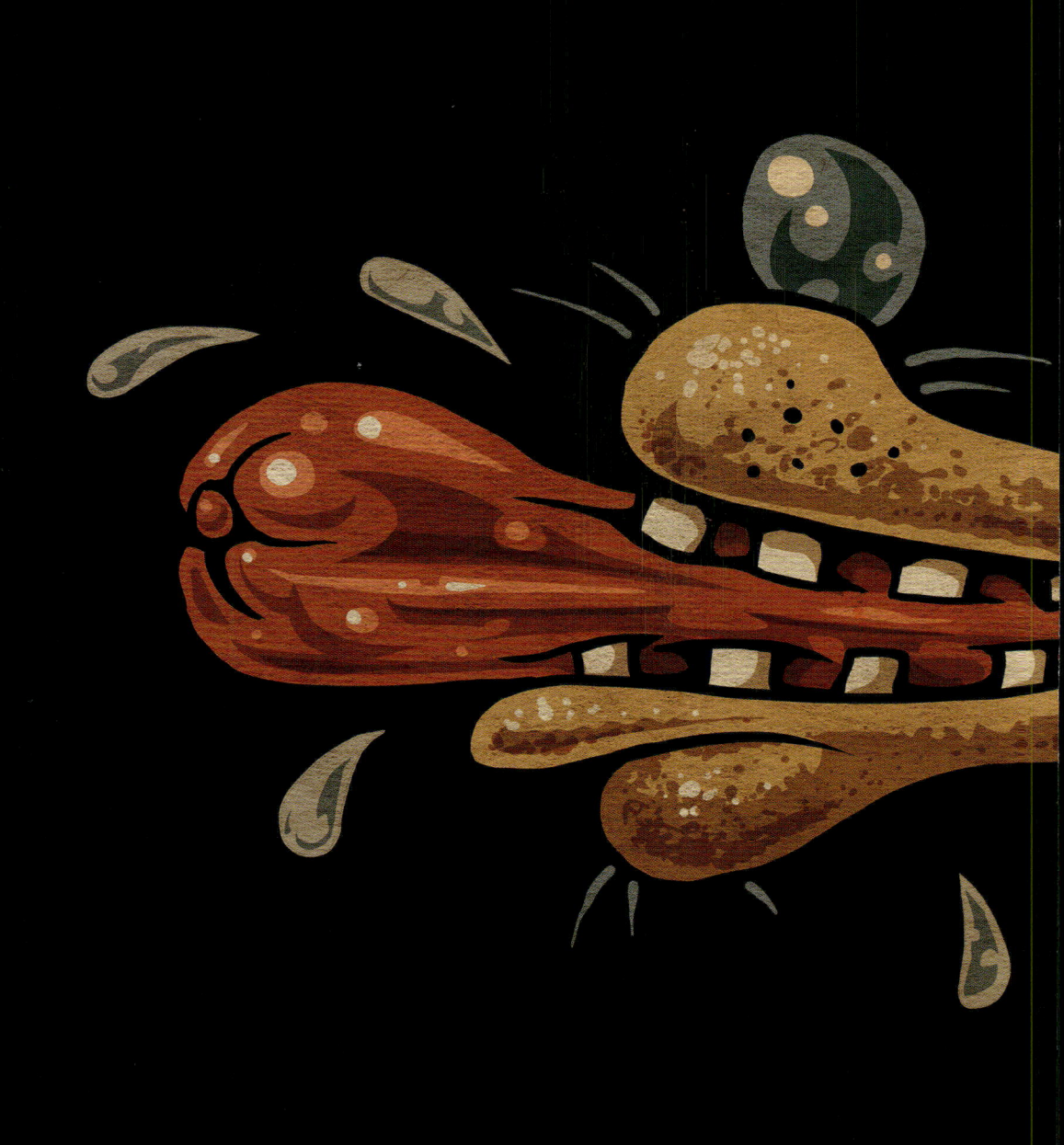

CHAPTER 6

Rejoice and Shake Ass

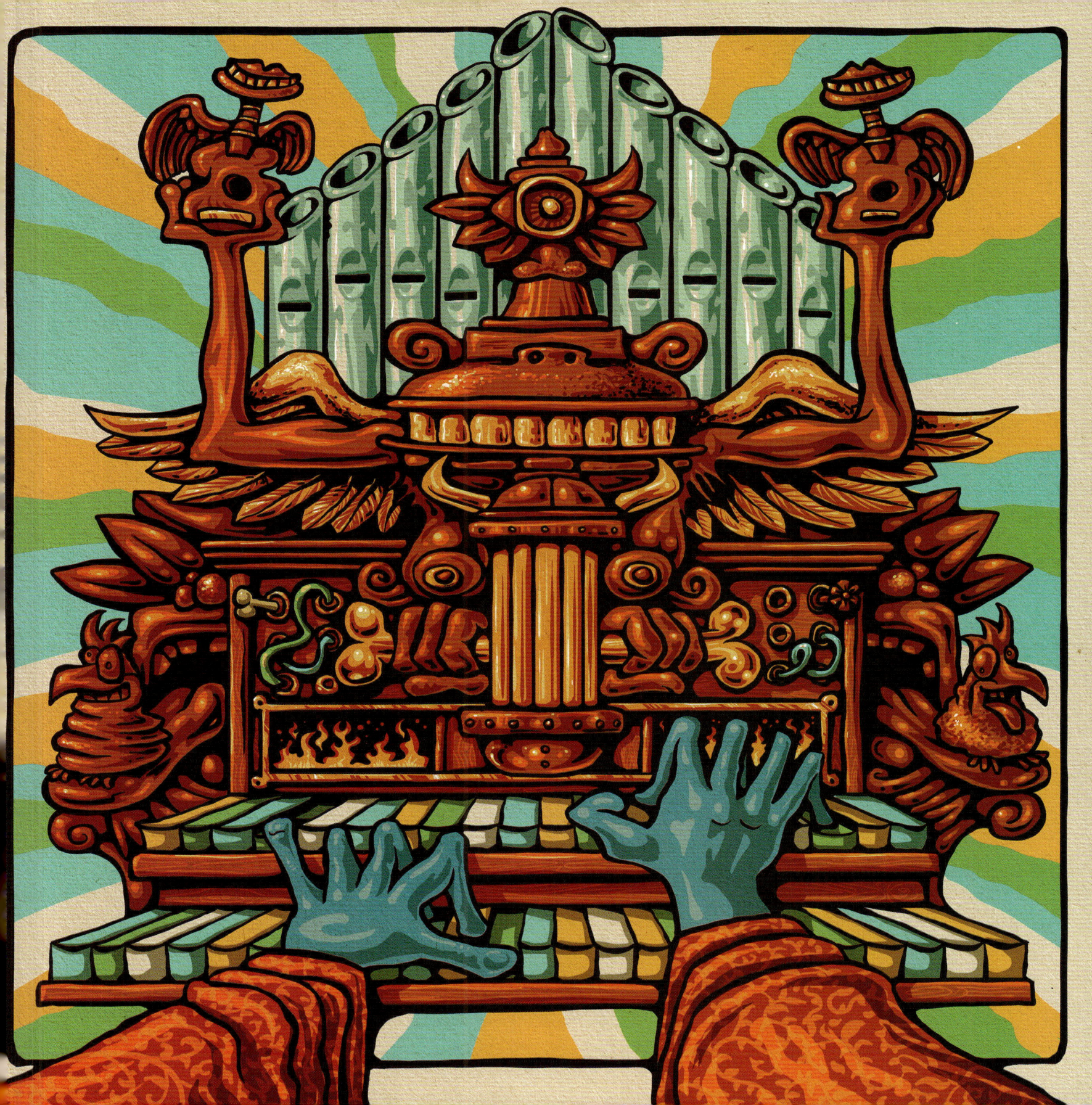

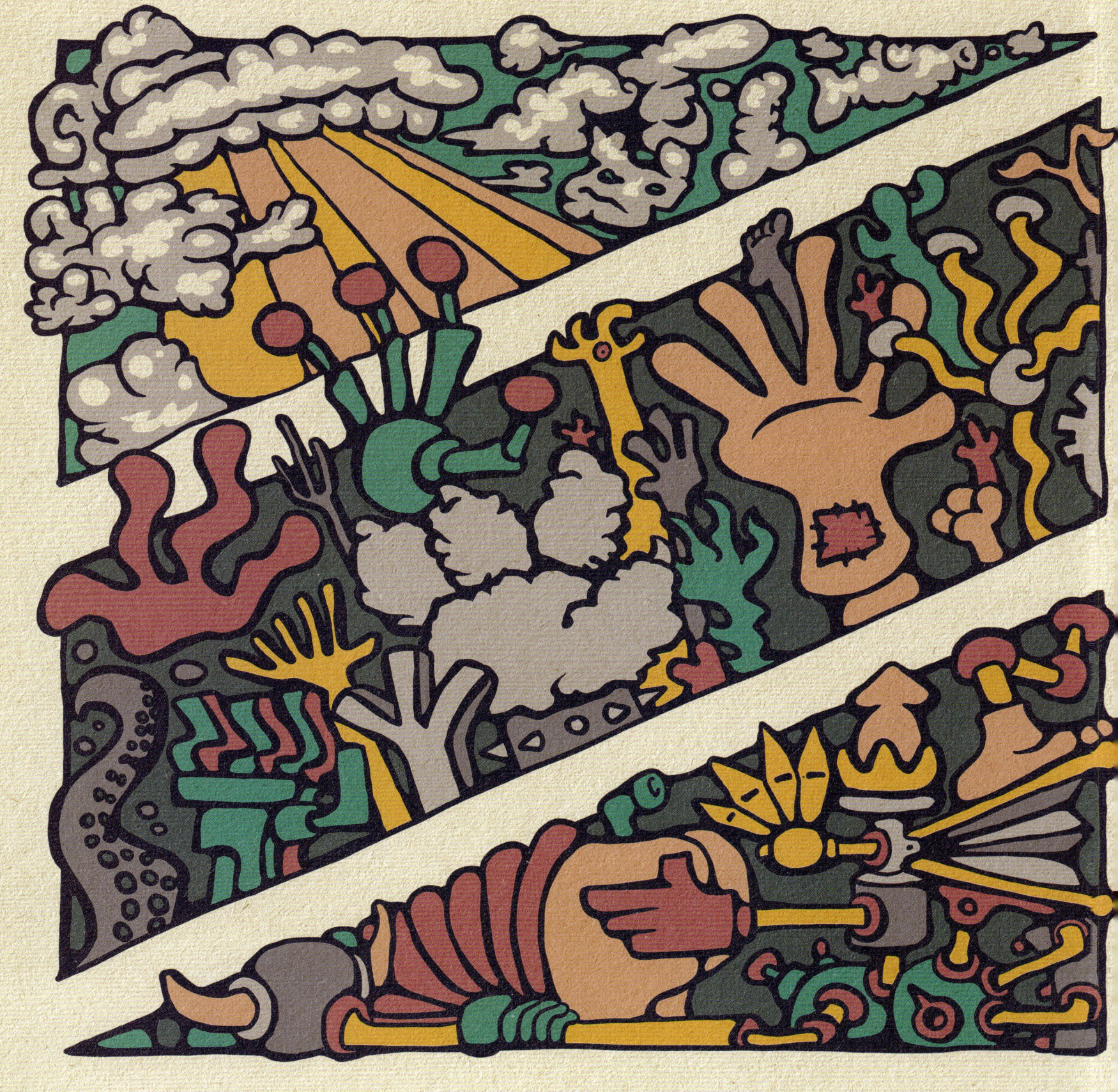

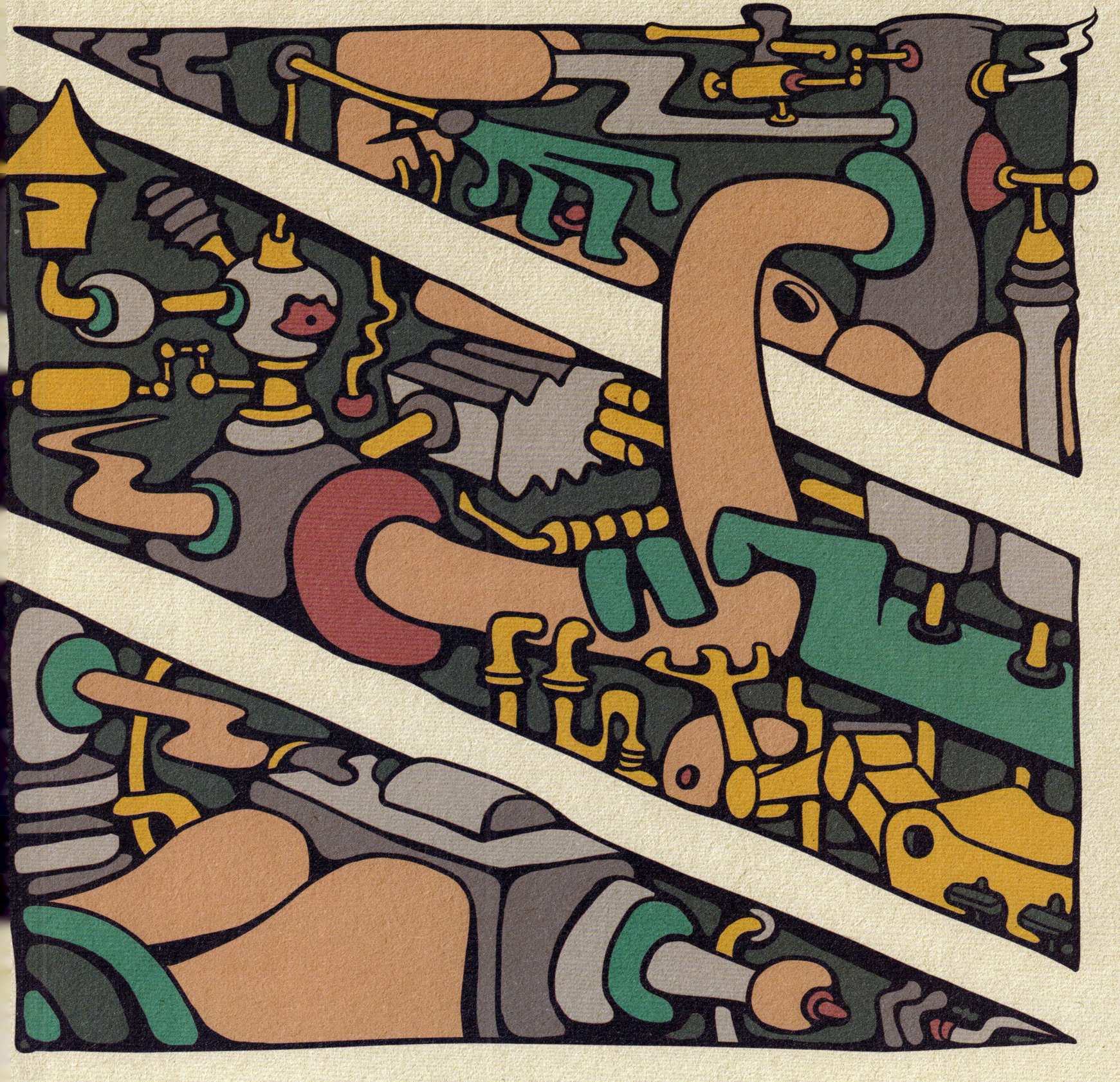

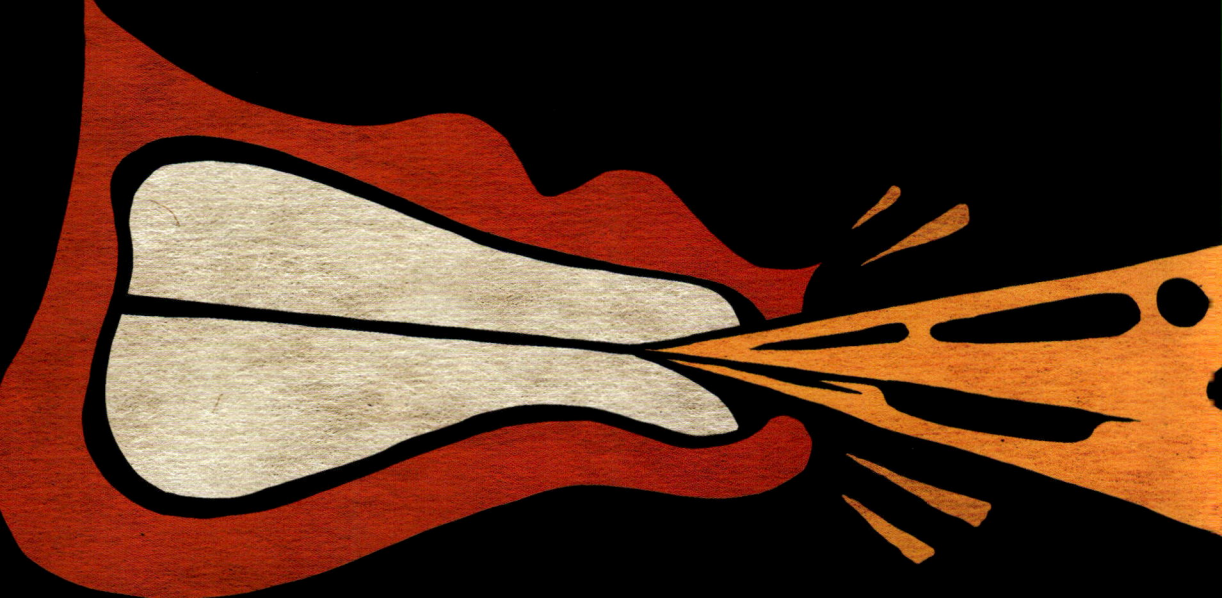

CHAPTER 7

She Rip Spandex

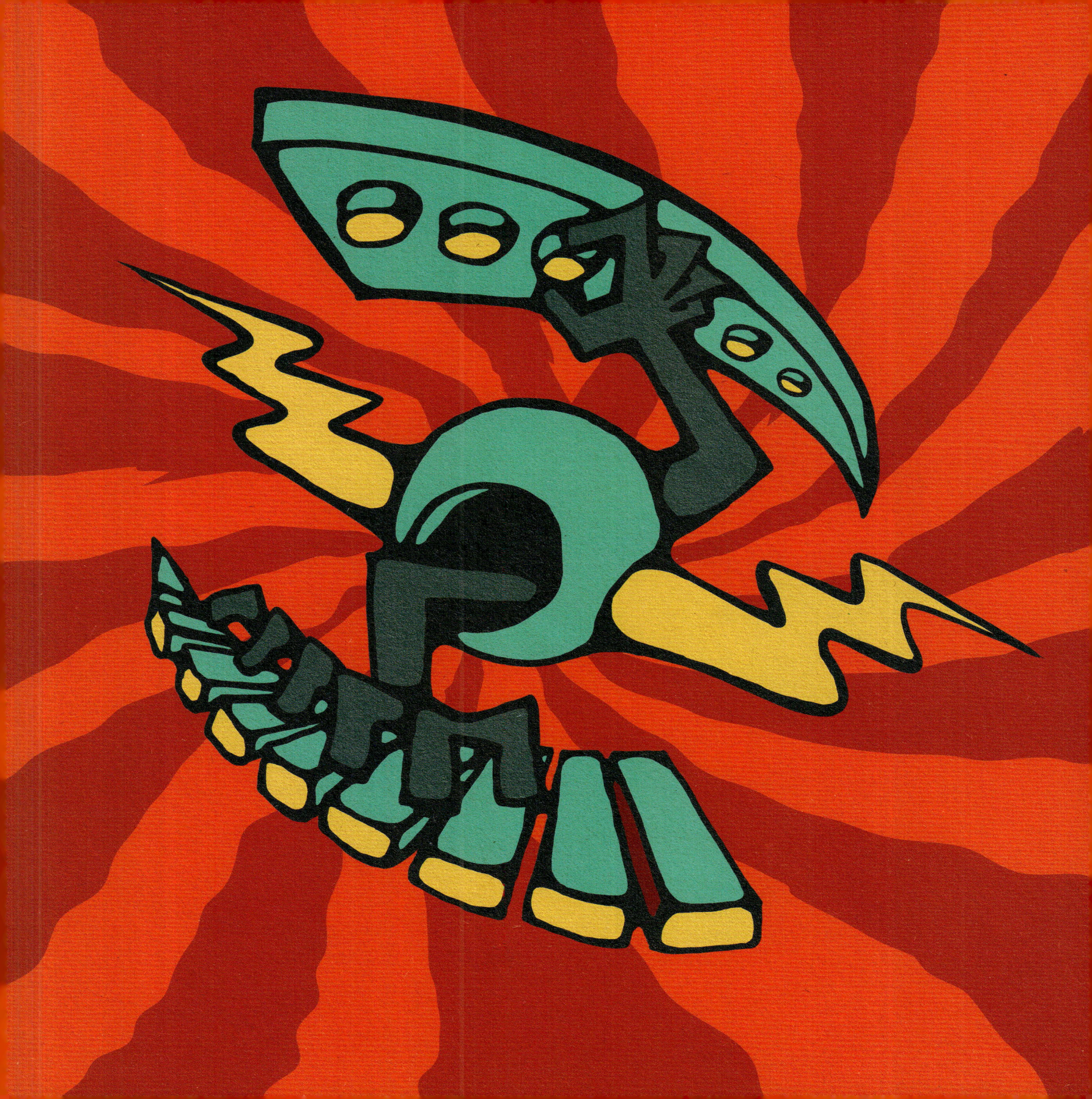

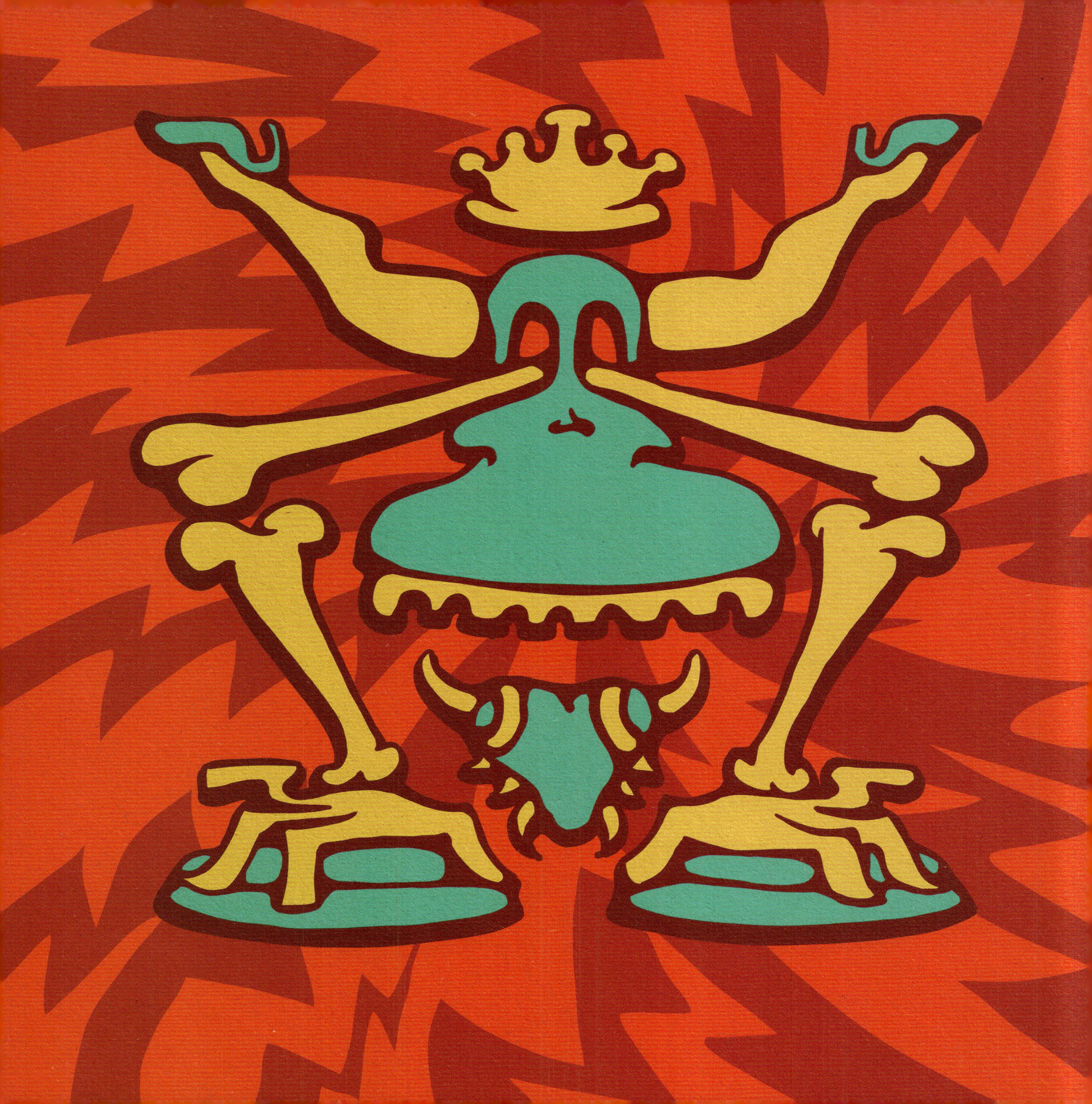

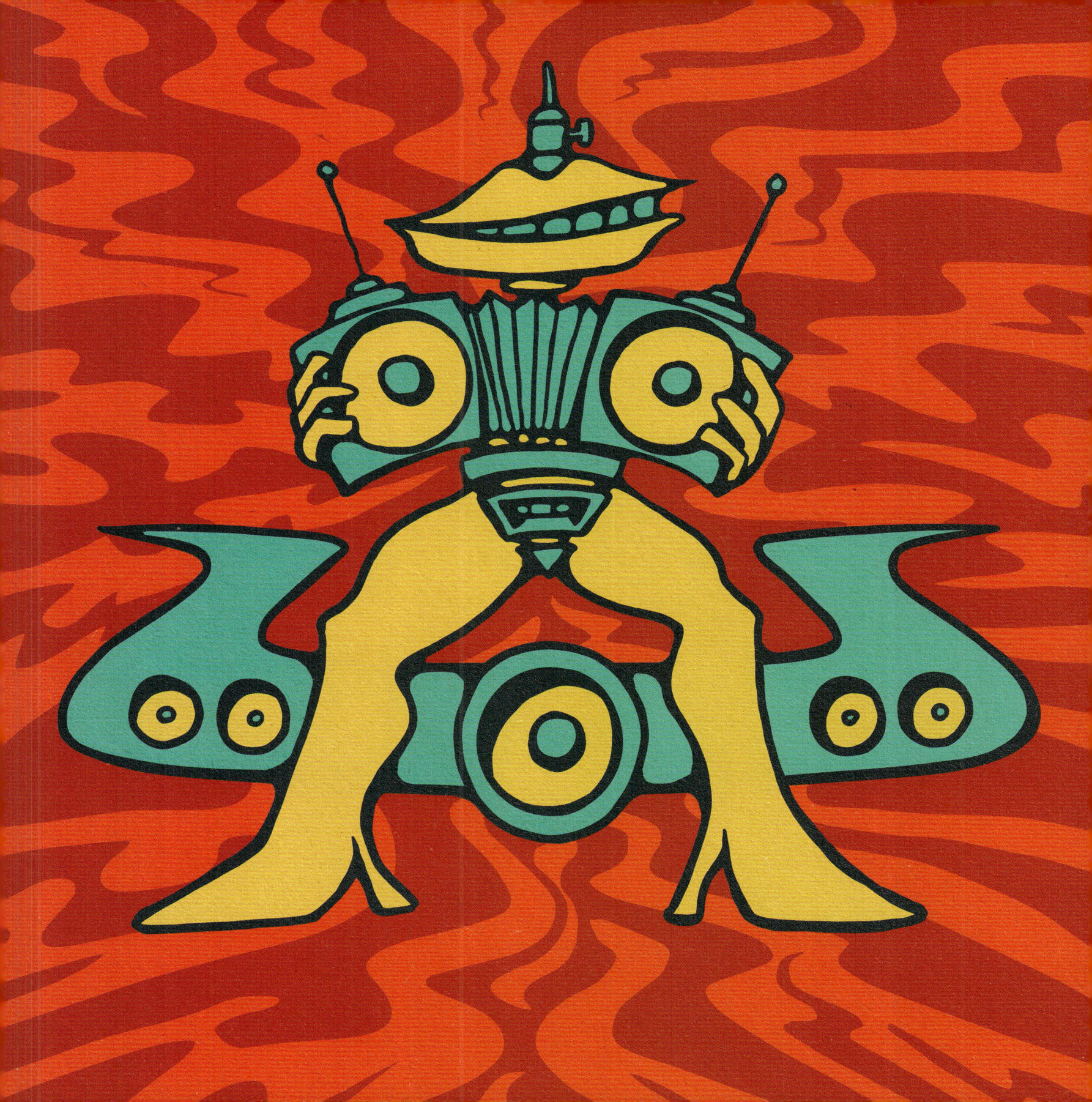

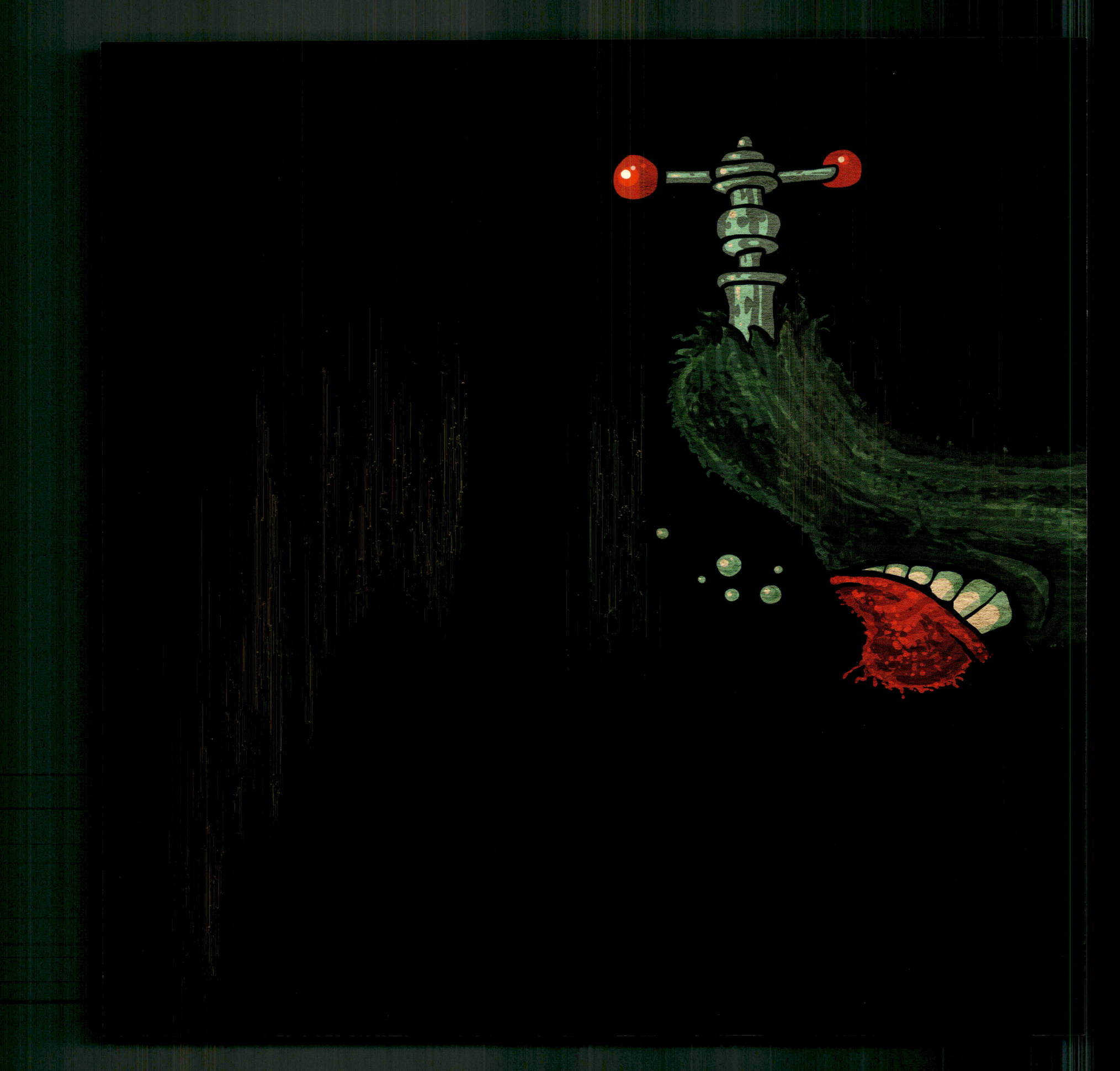

CHAPTER 8

The Laundrette Conspiracy

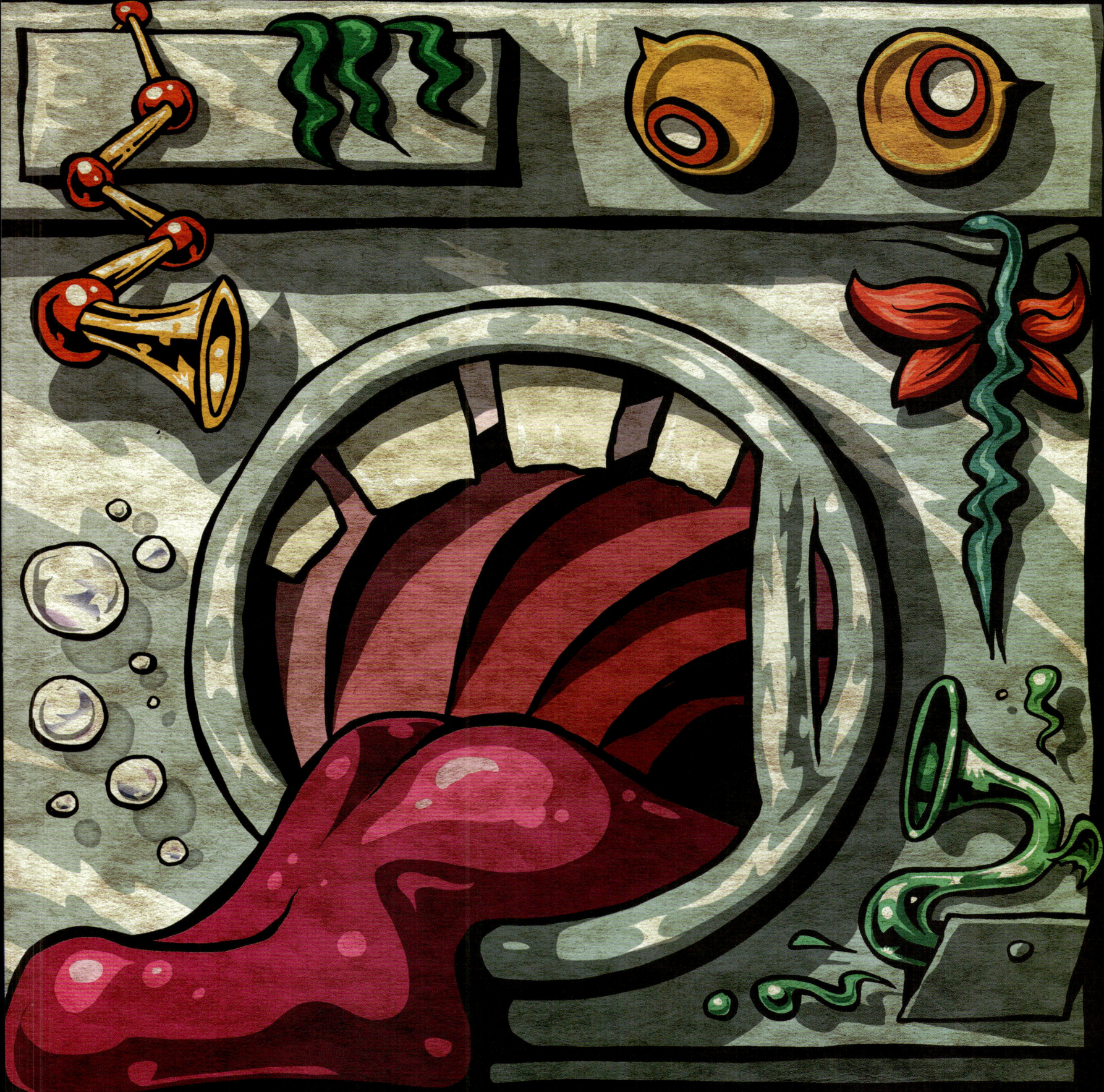

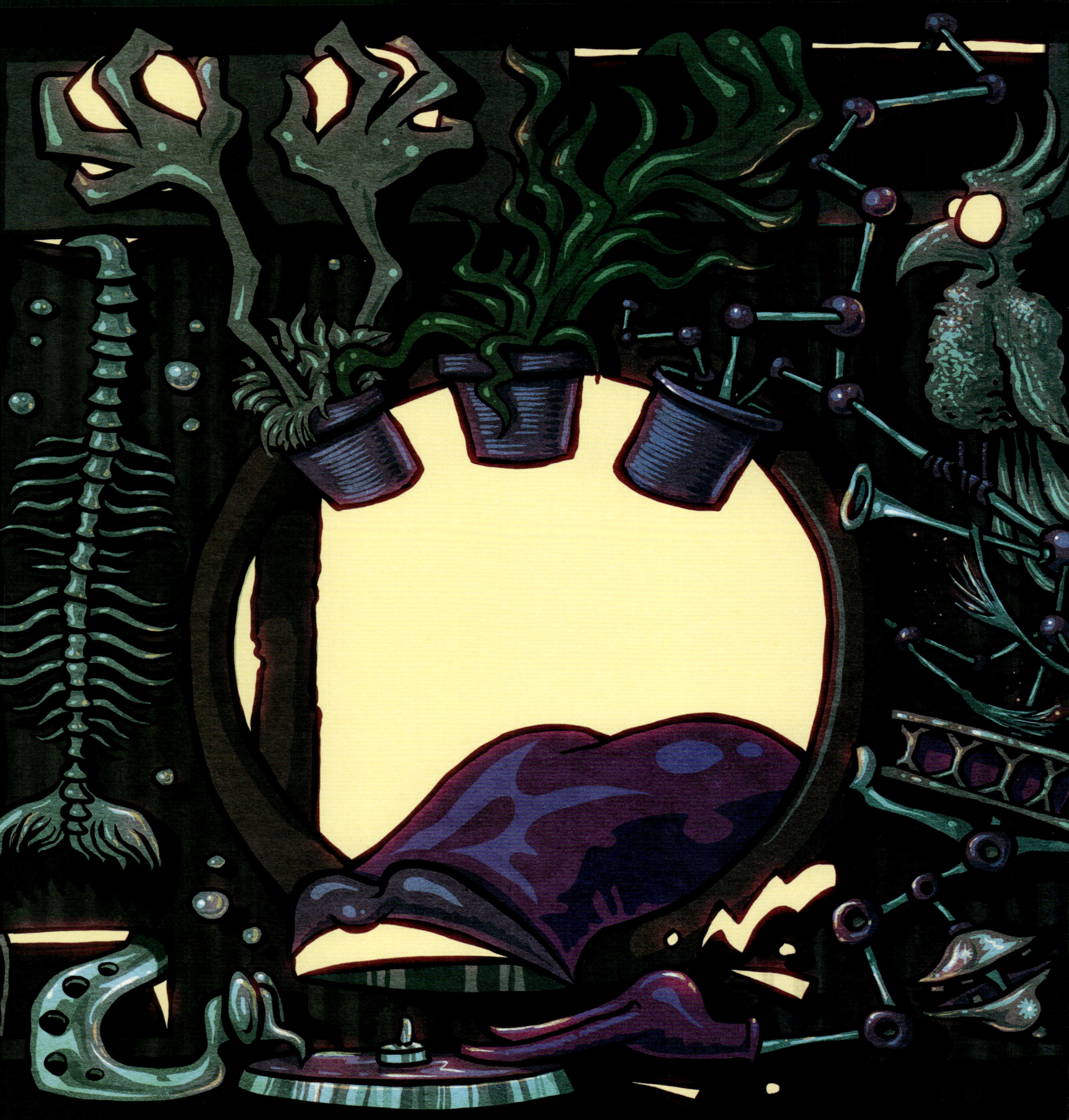

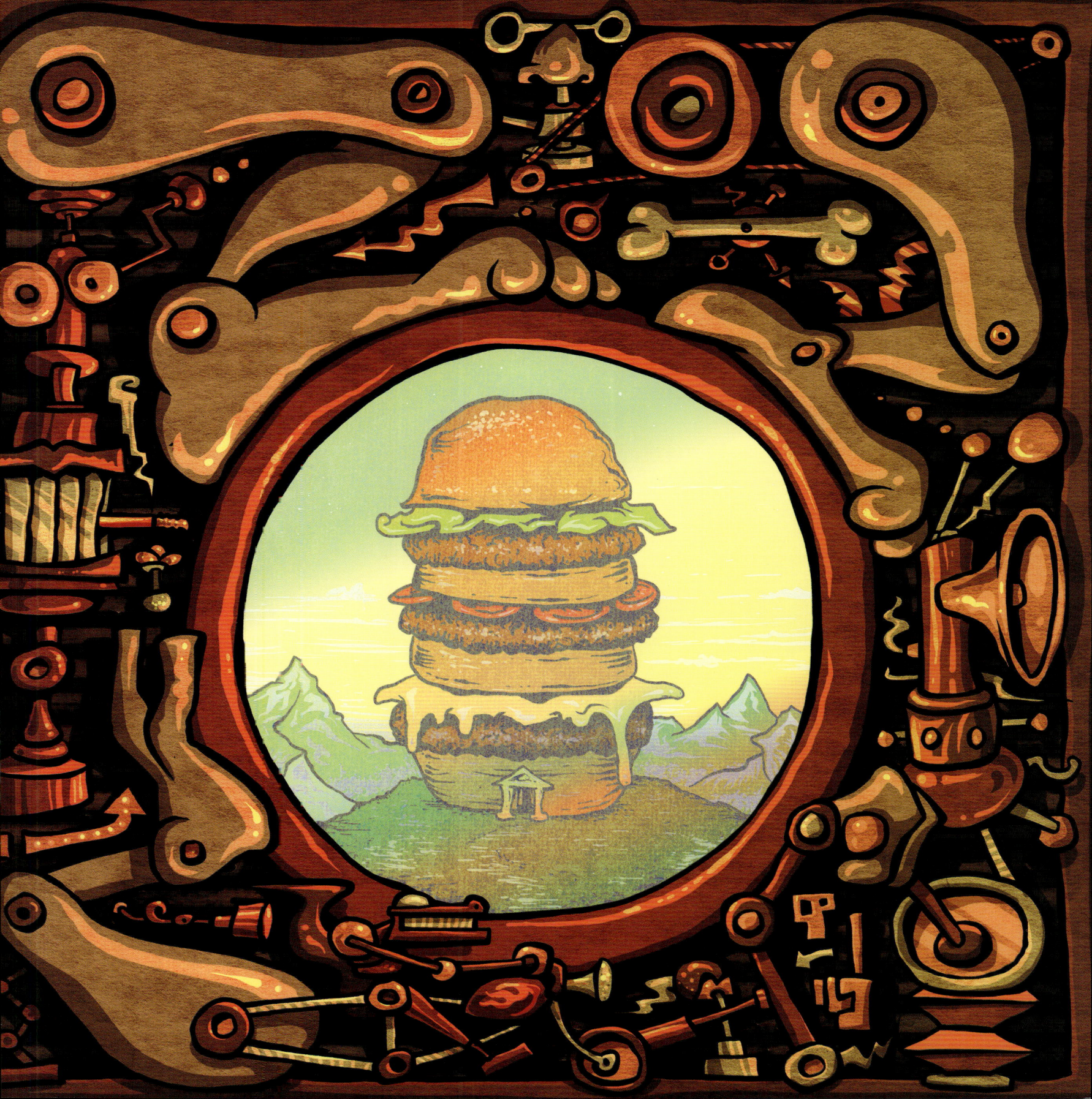

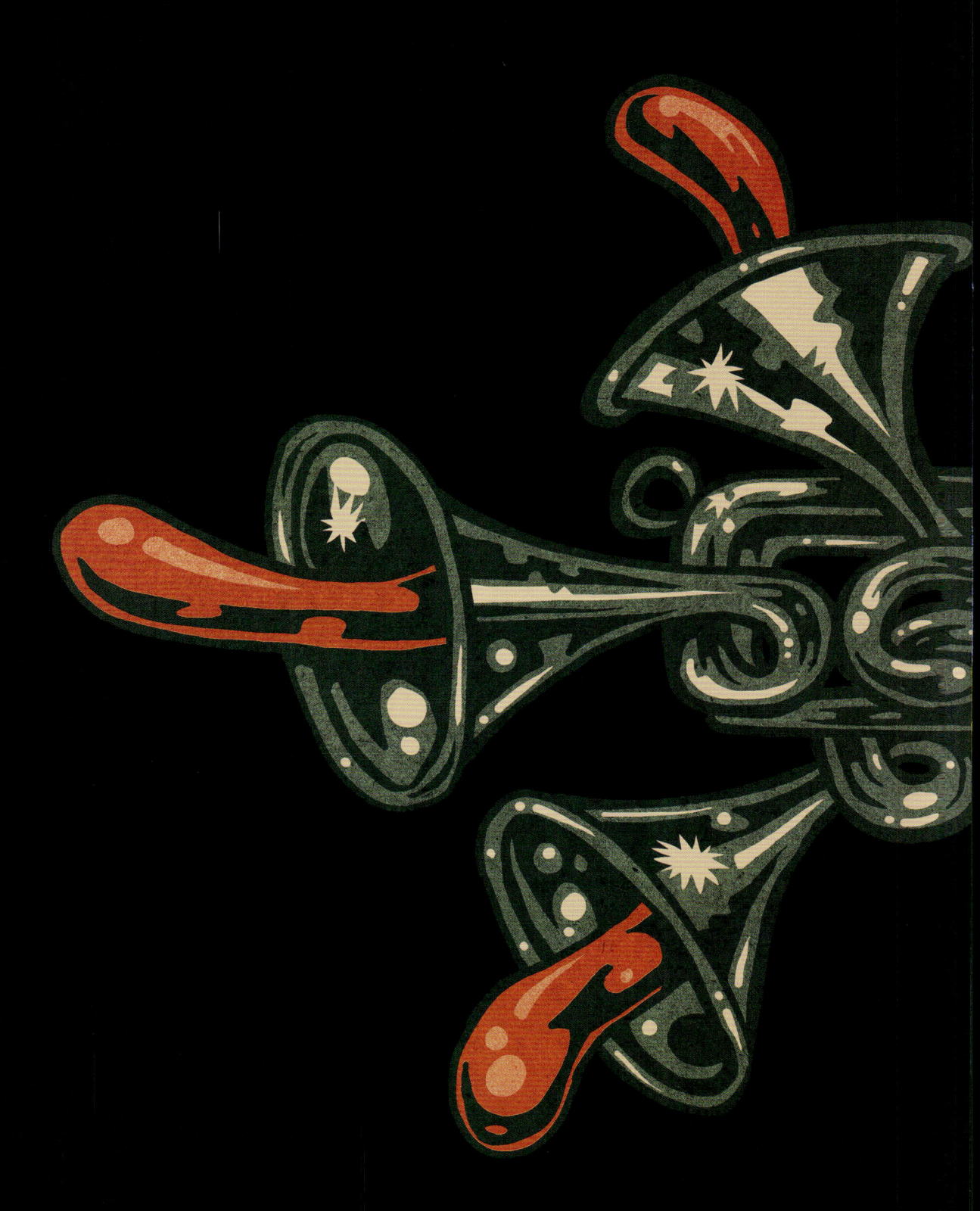

CHAPTER 9

Moose Knuckle Sandwich

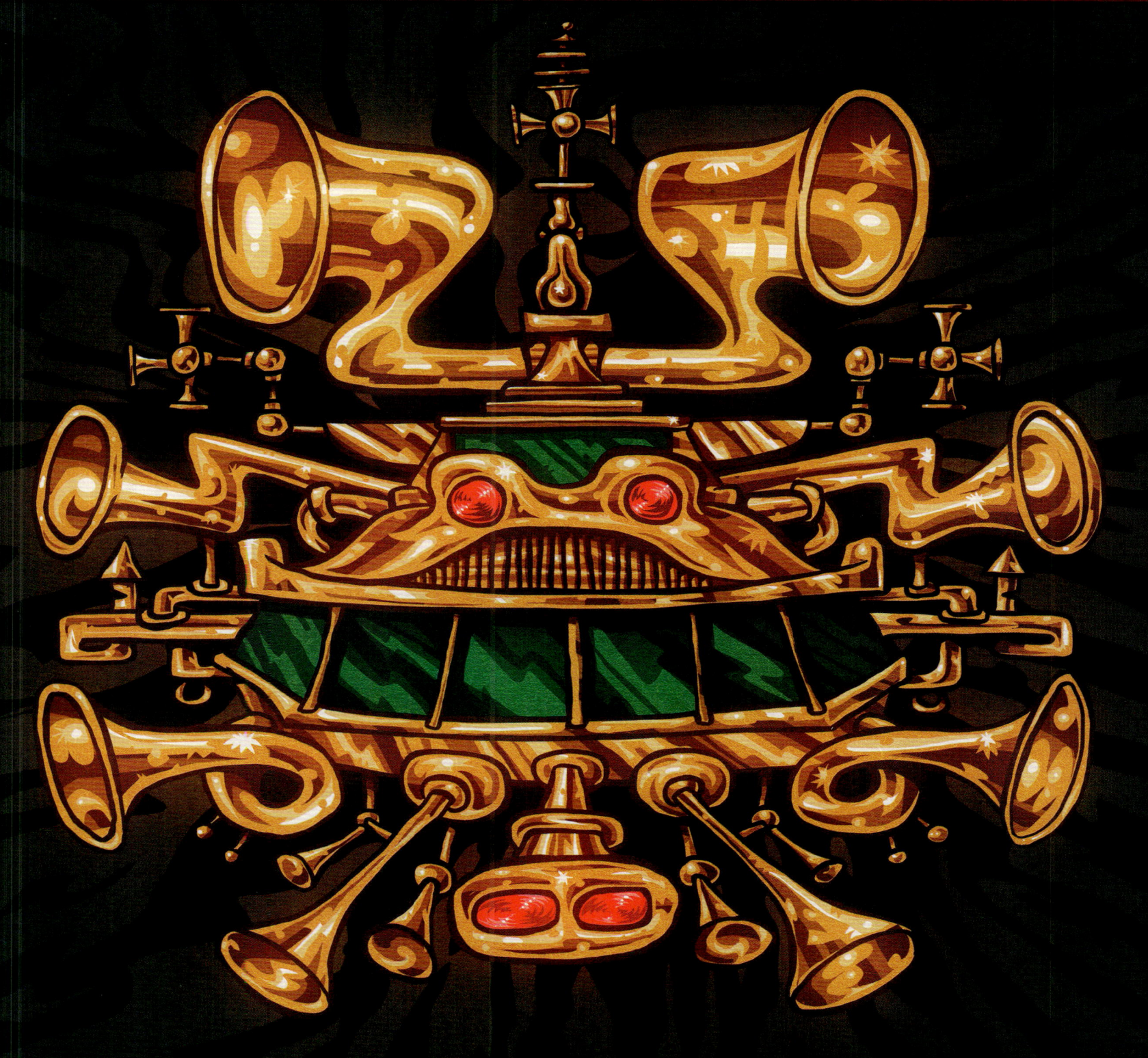

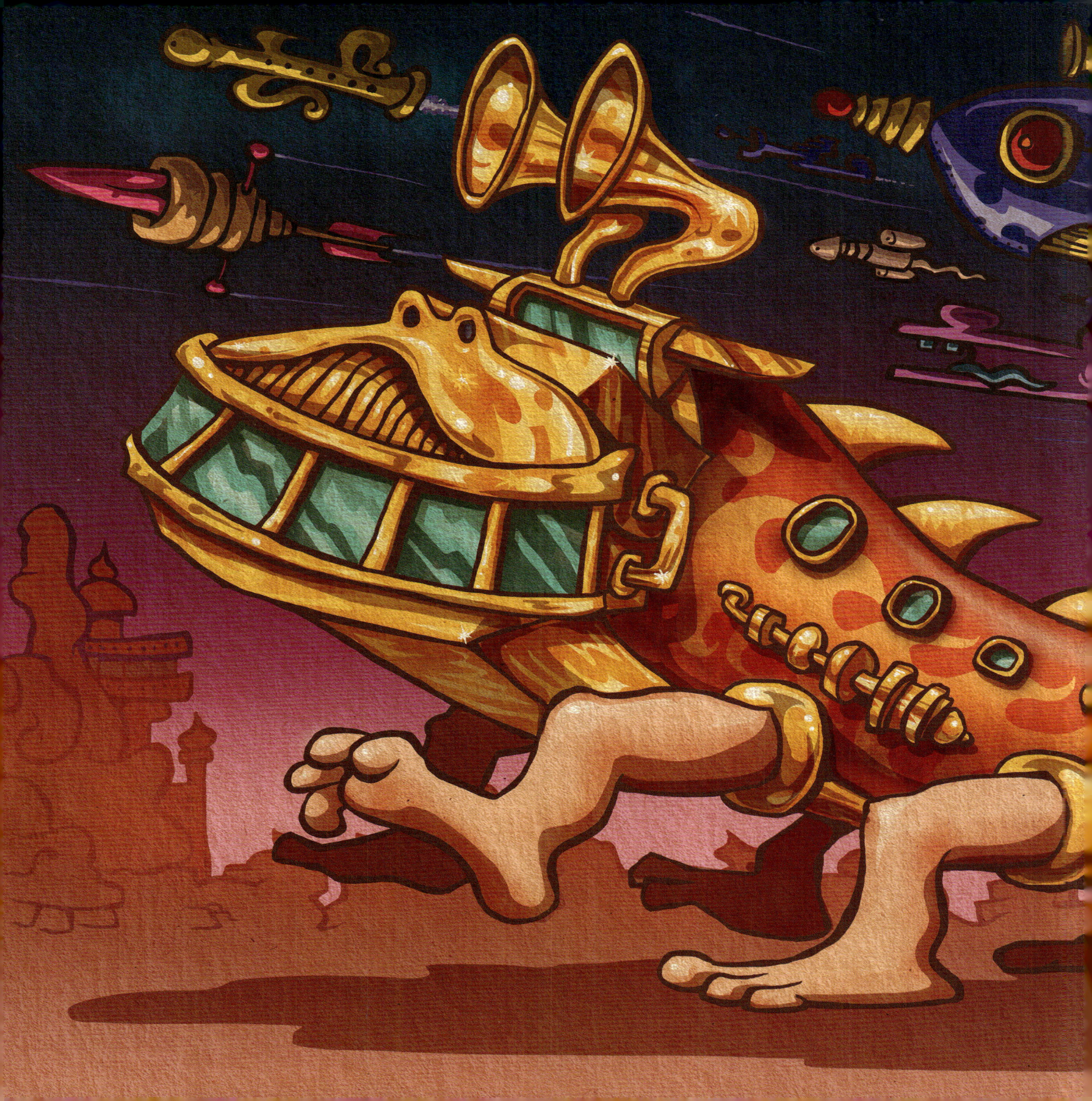

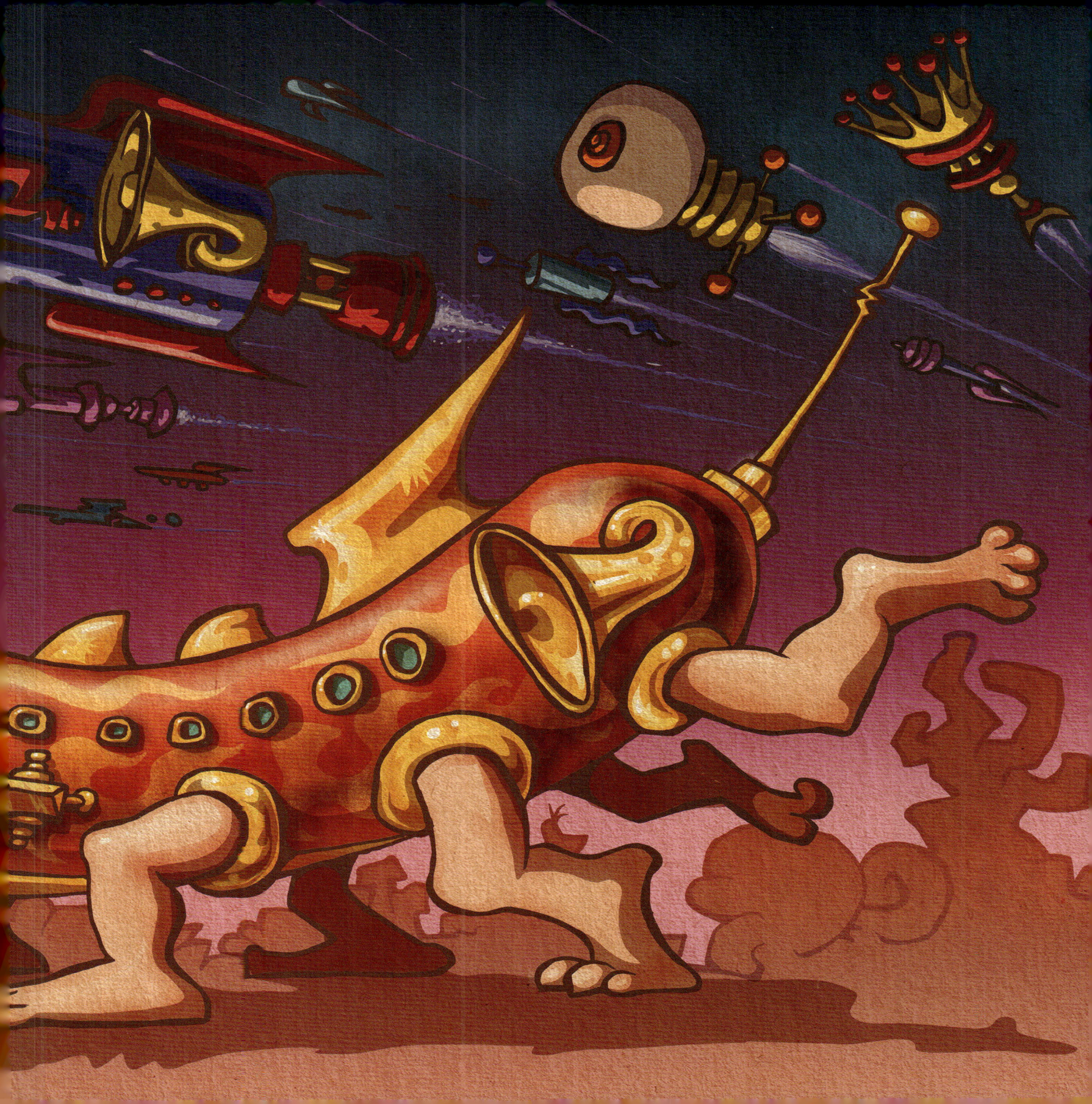

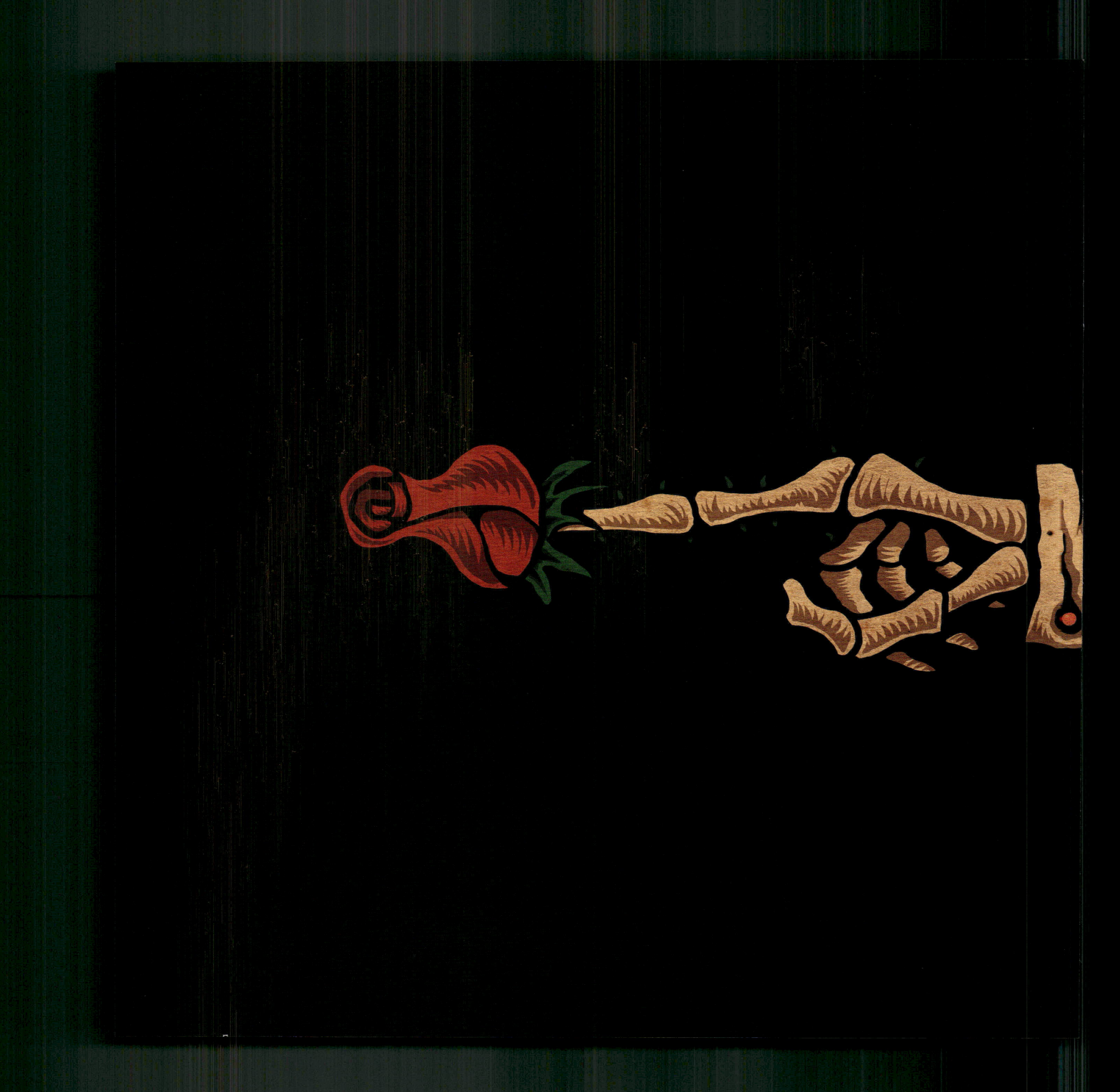

CHAPTER 10

Knead us to Temptation

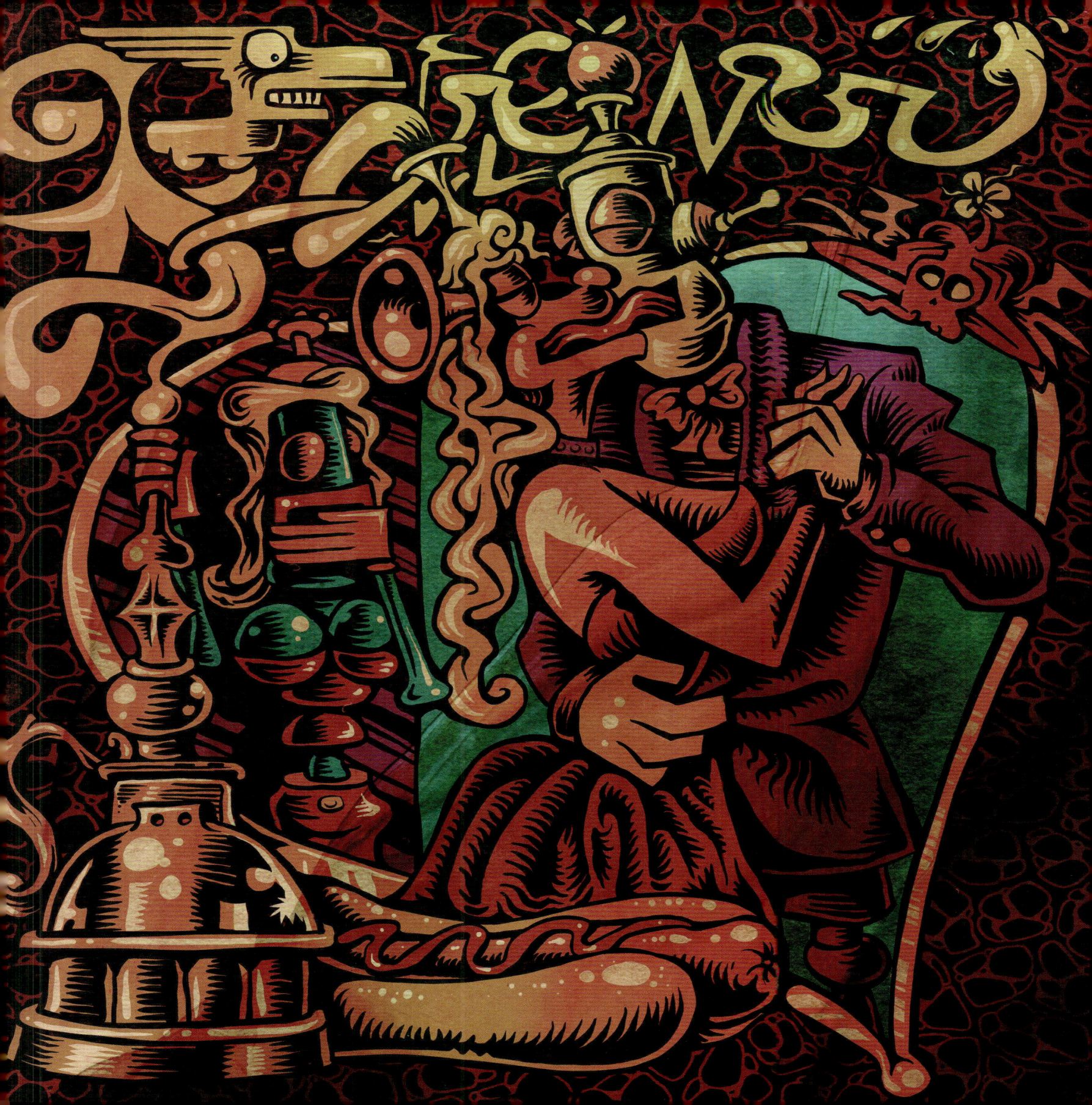

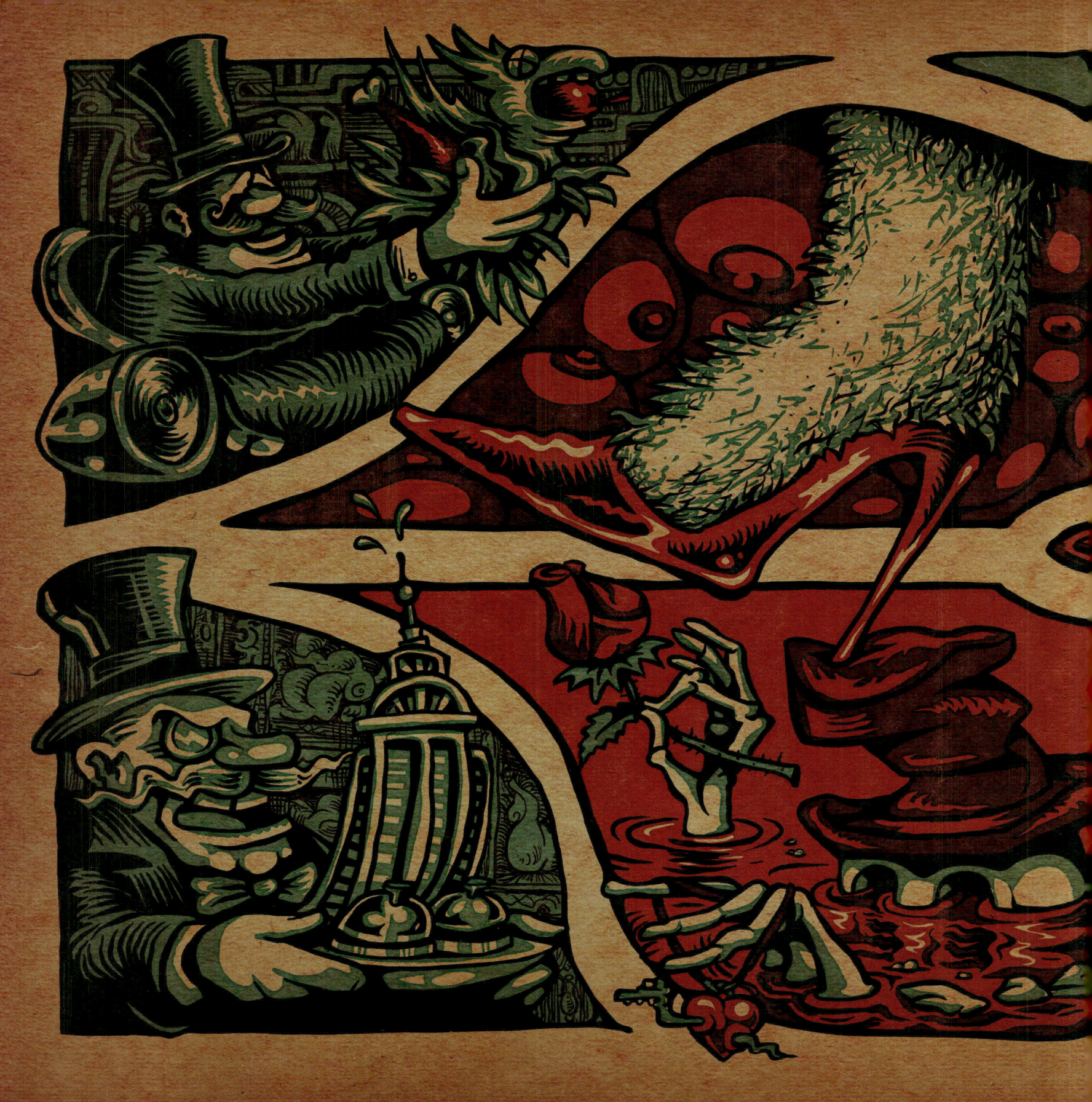

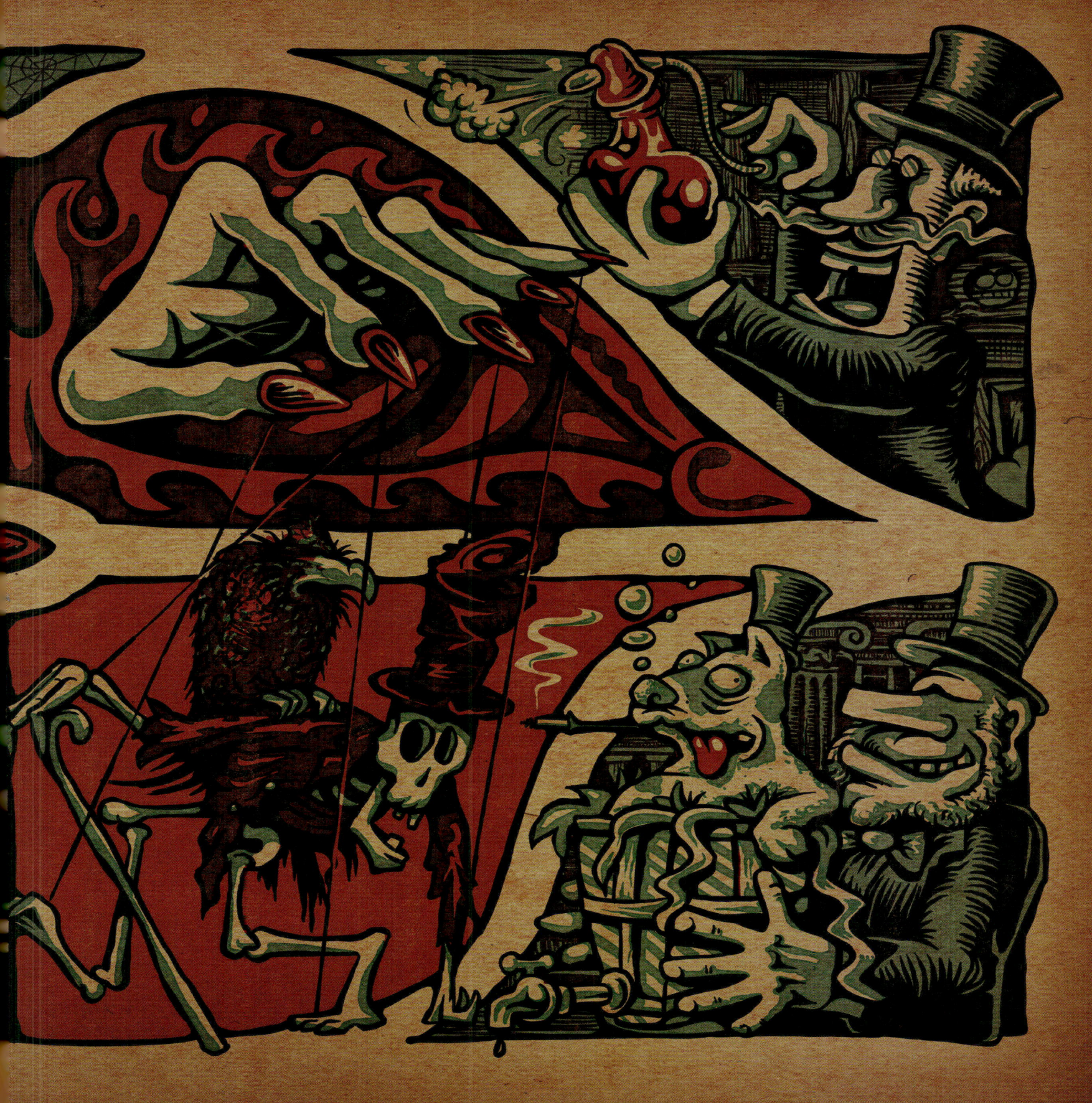

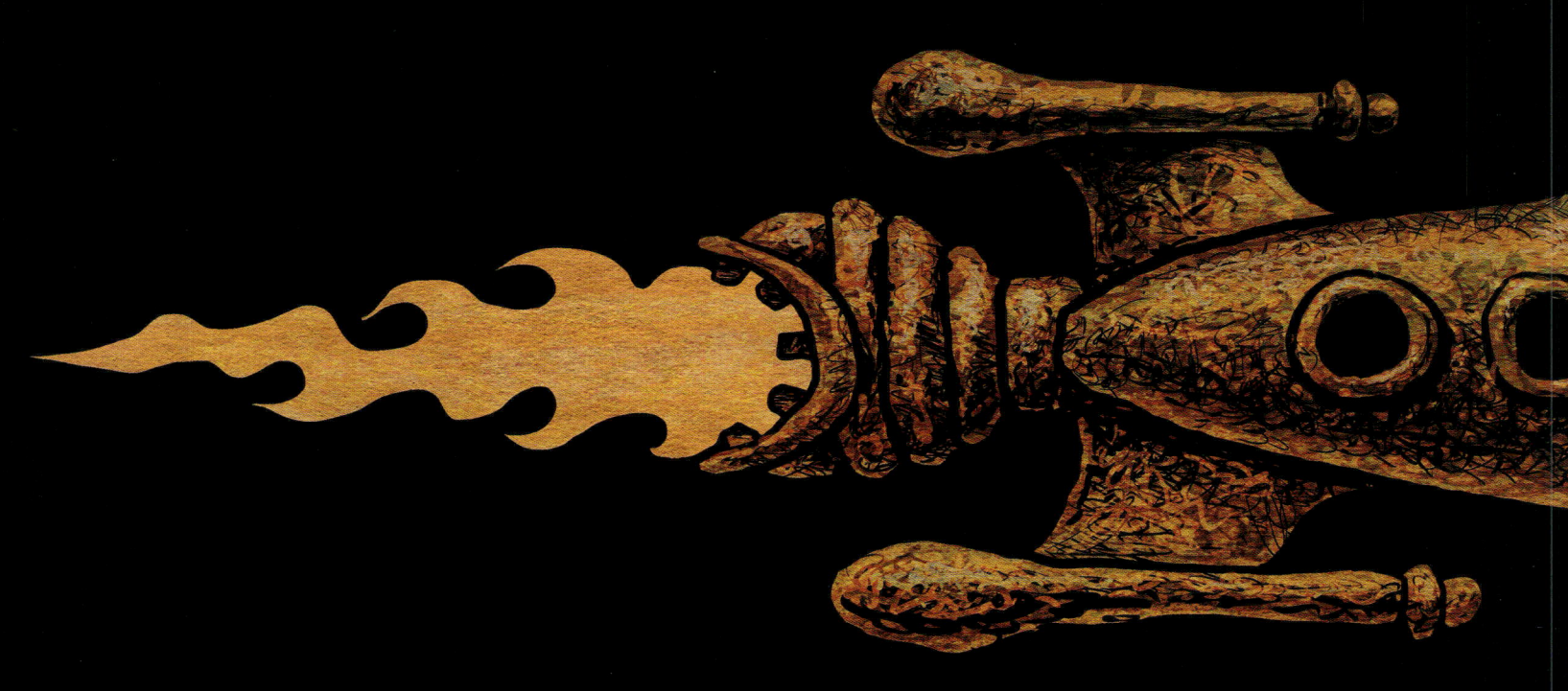

CHAPTER 11

Chili con Carnage

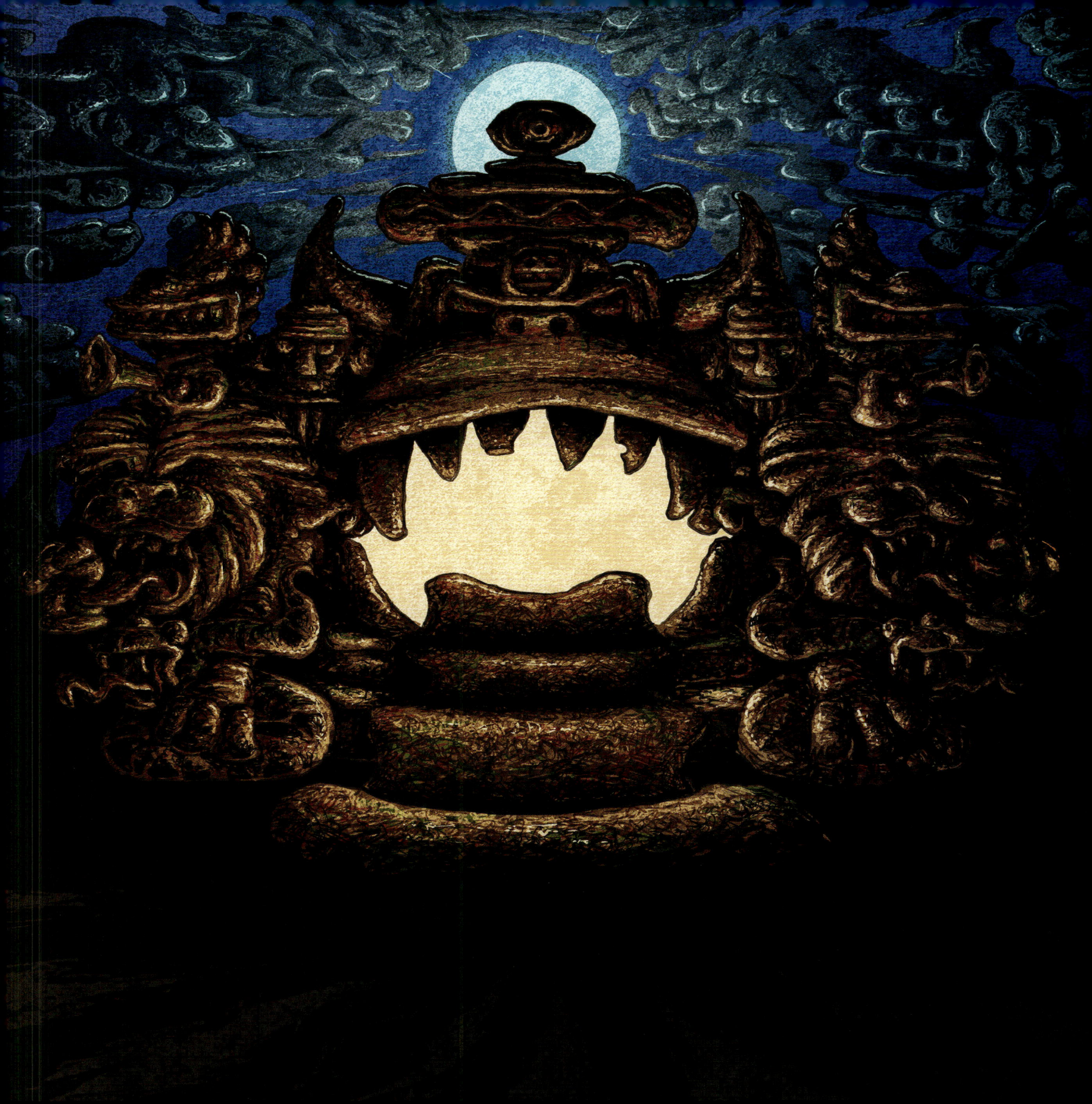

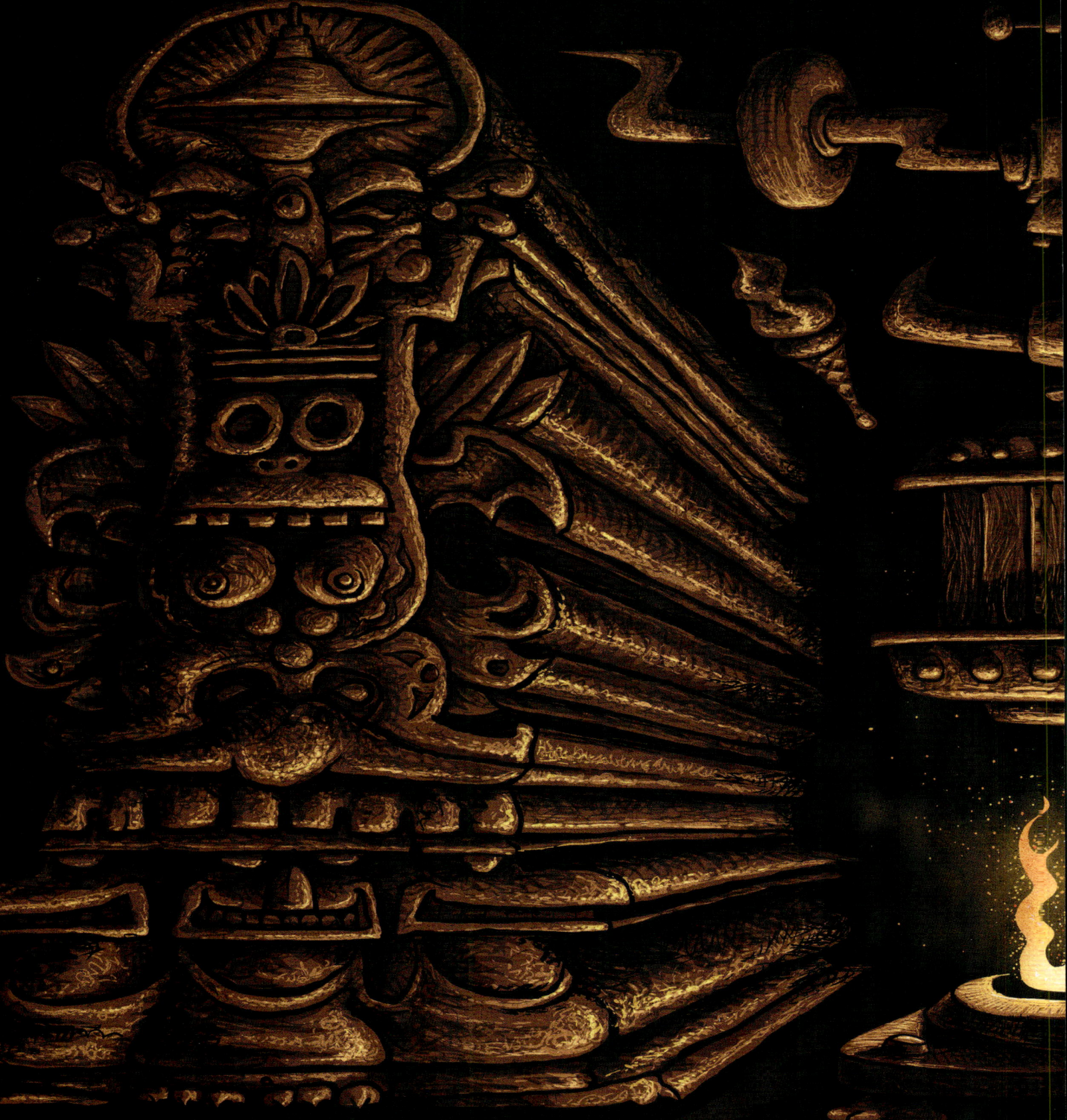

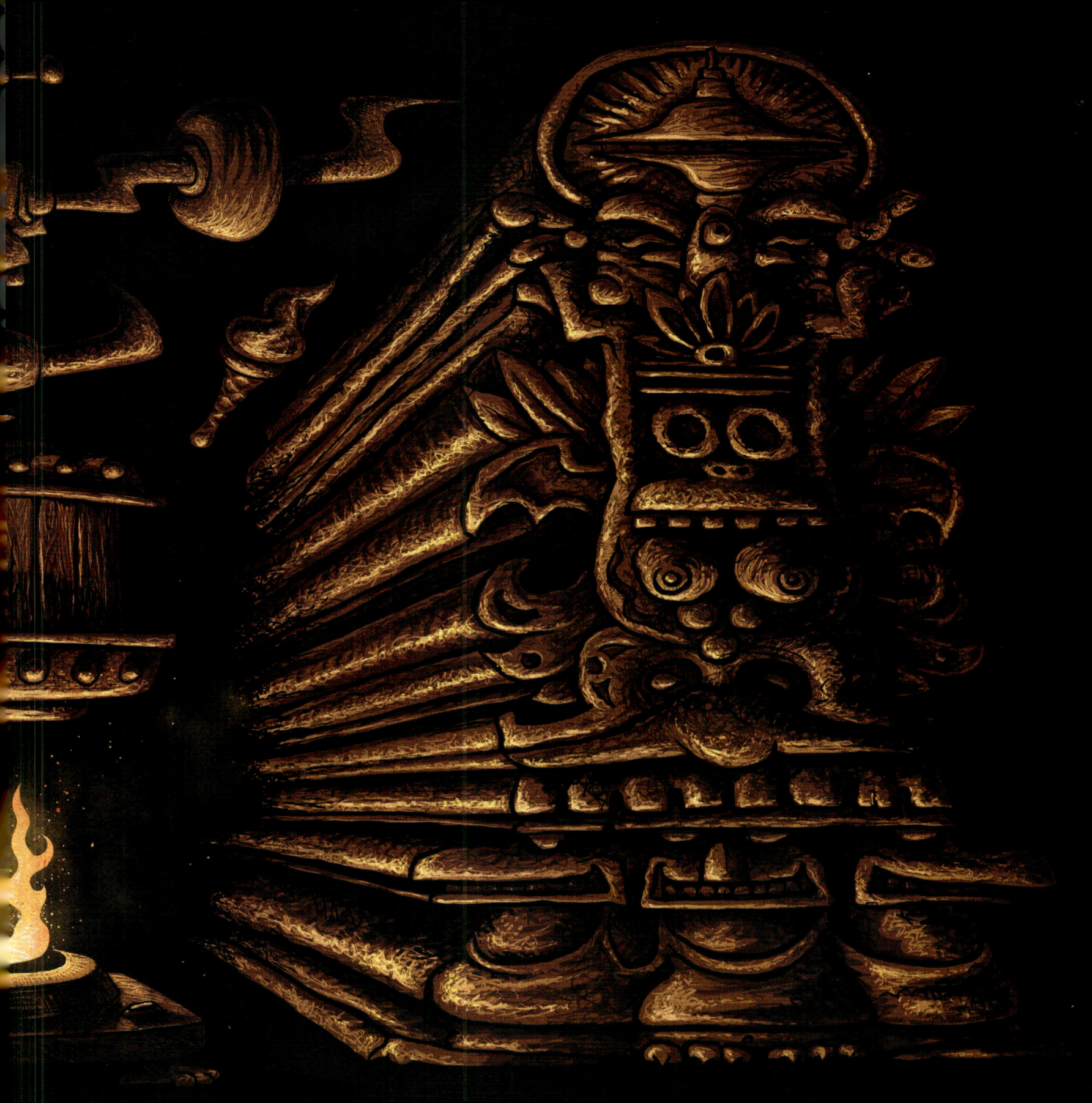

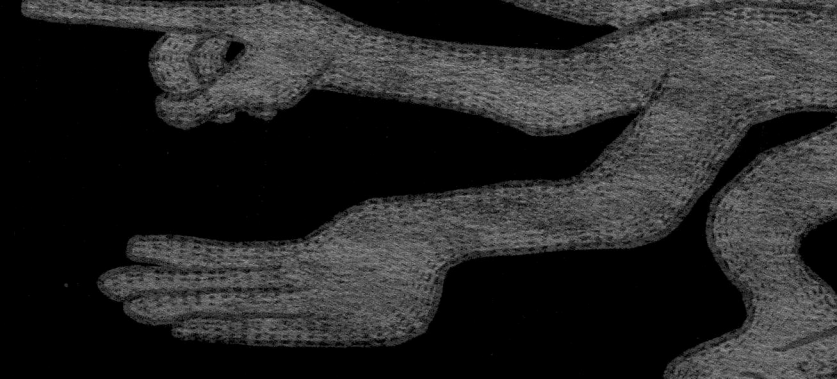

CHAPTER 12

Serendipity Blues

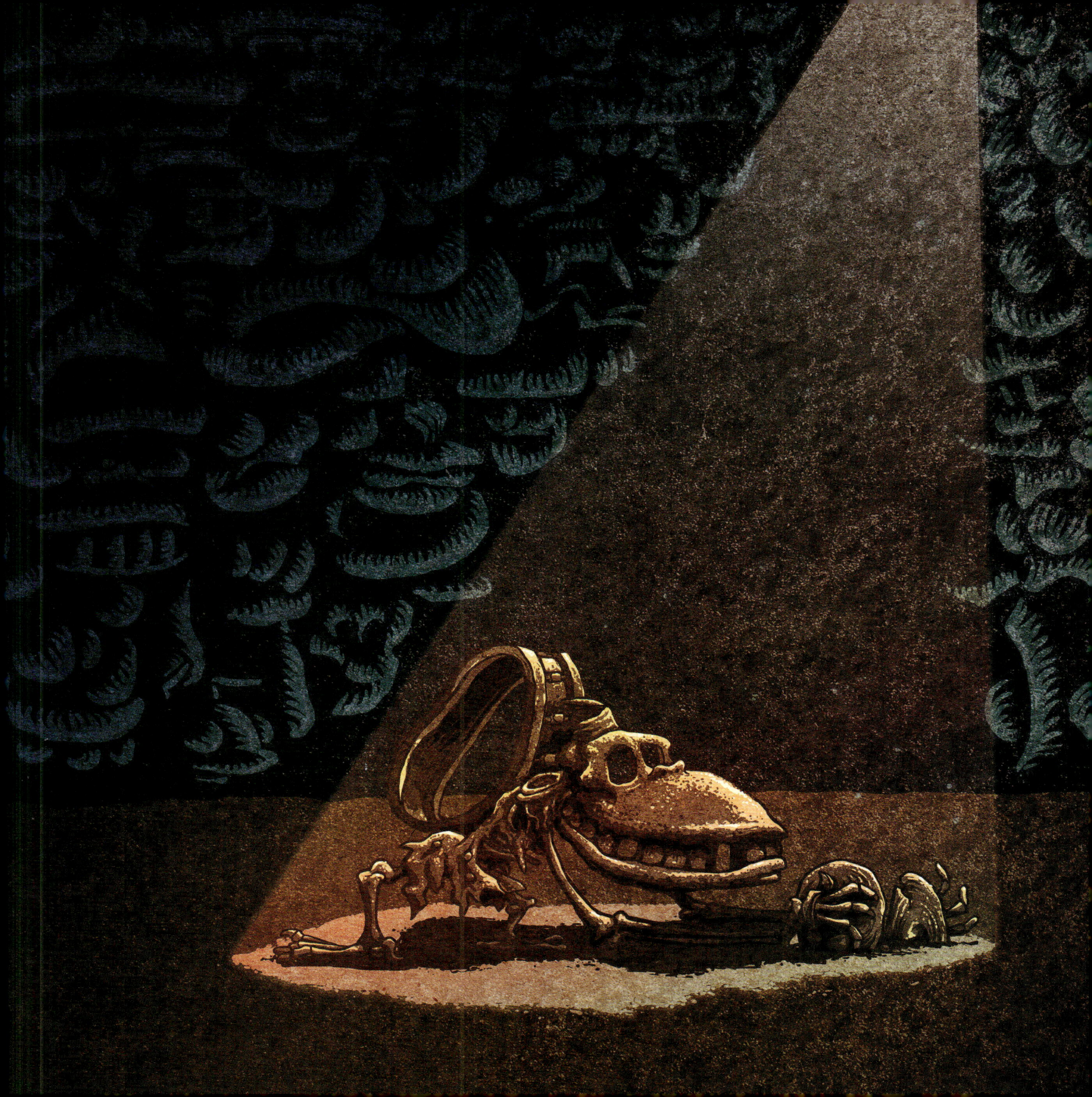

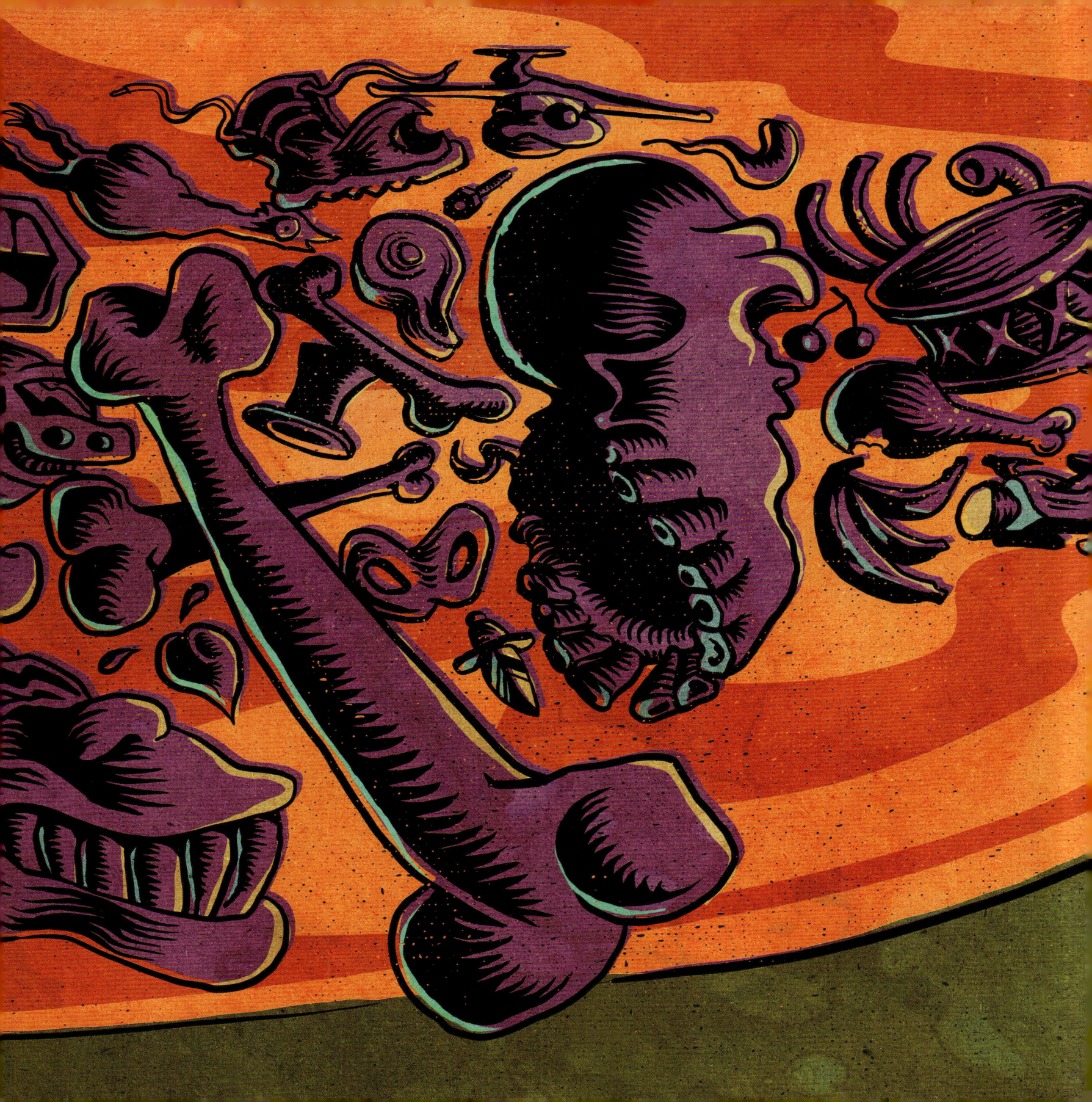

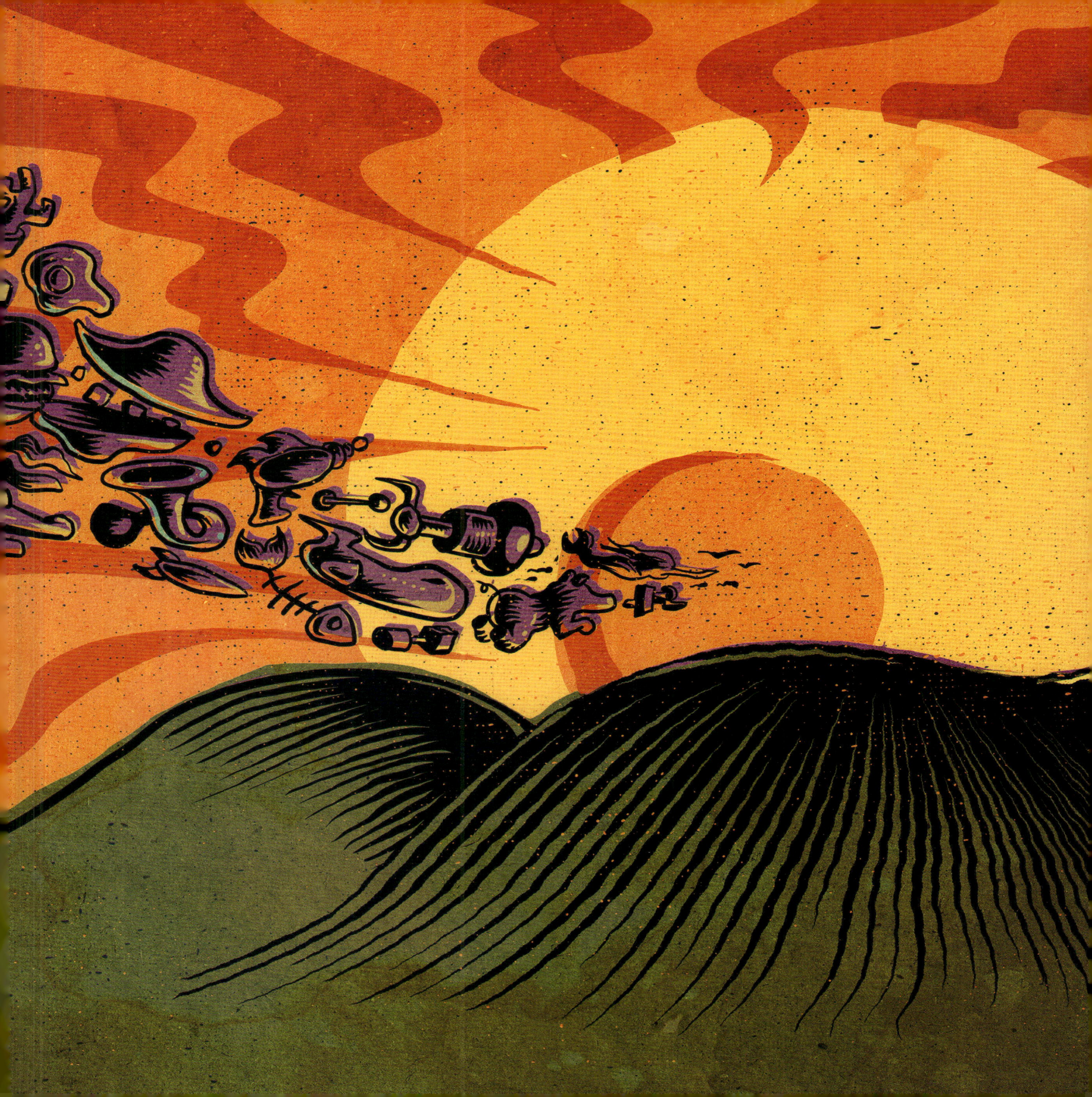

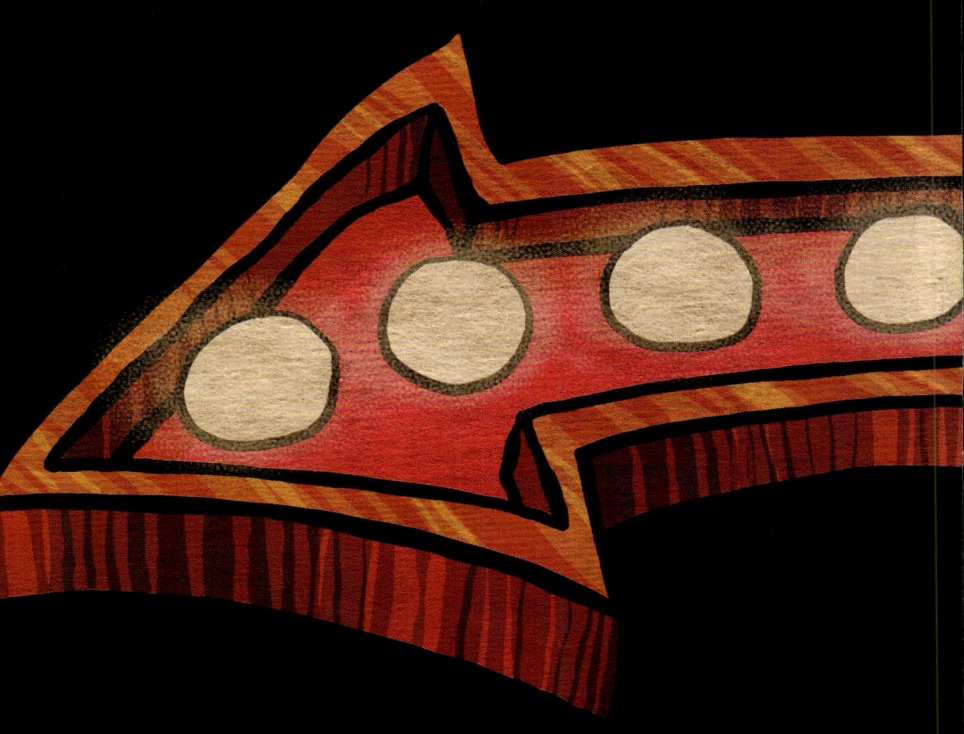

CHAPTER 13

Late Night Check-in at the Neon Tuxedo Hotel

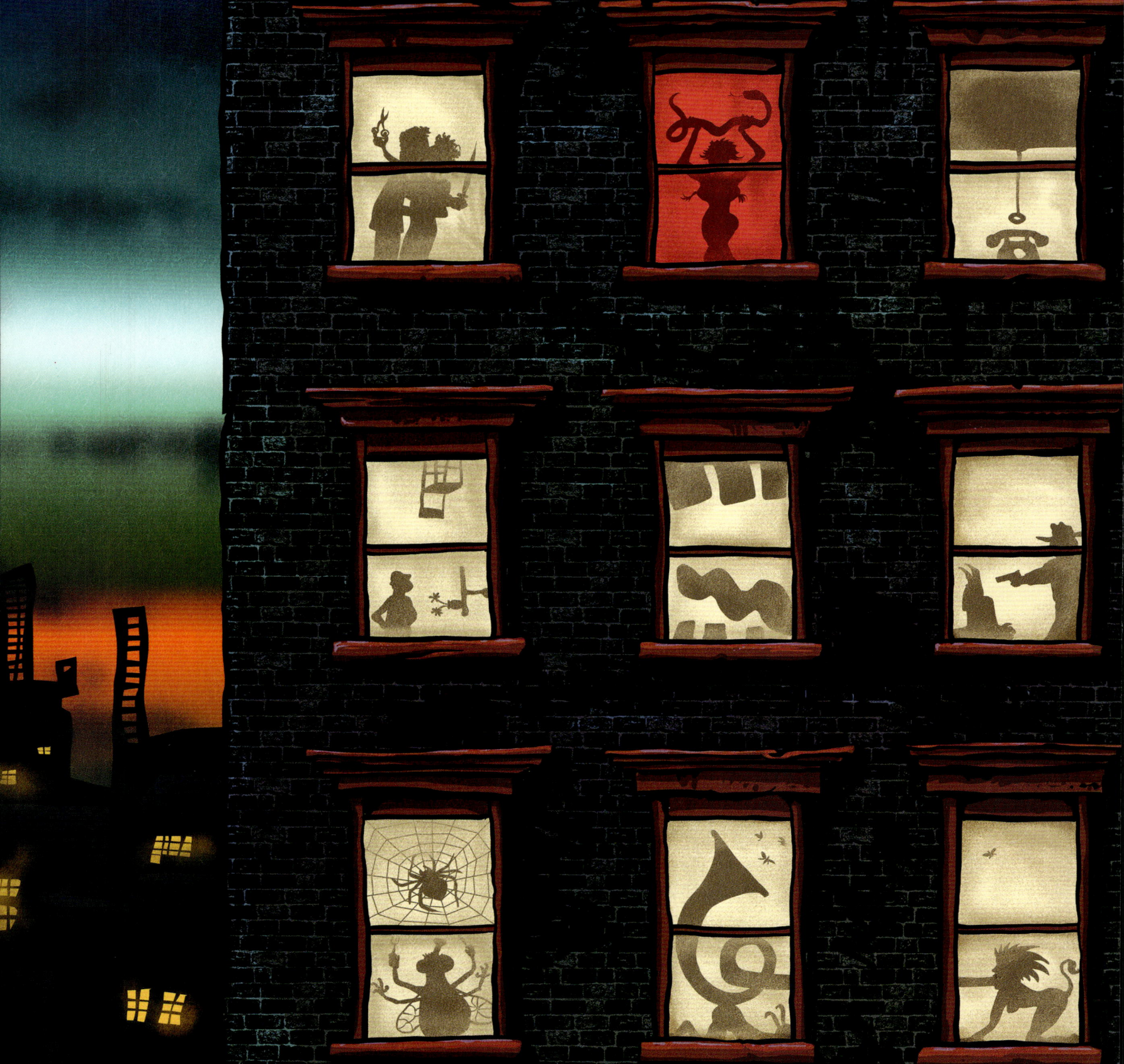

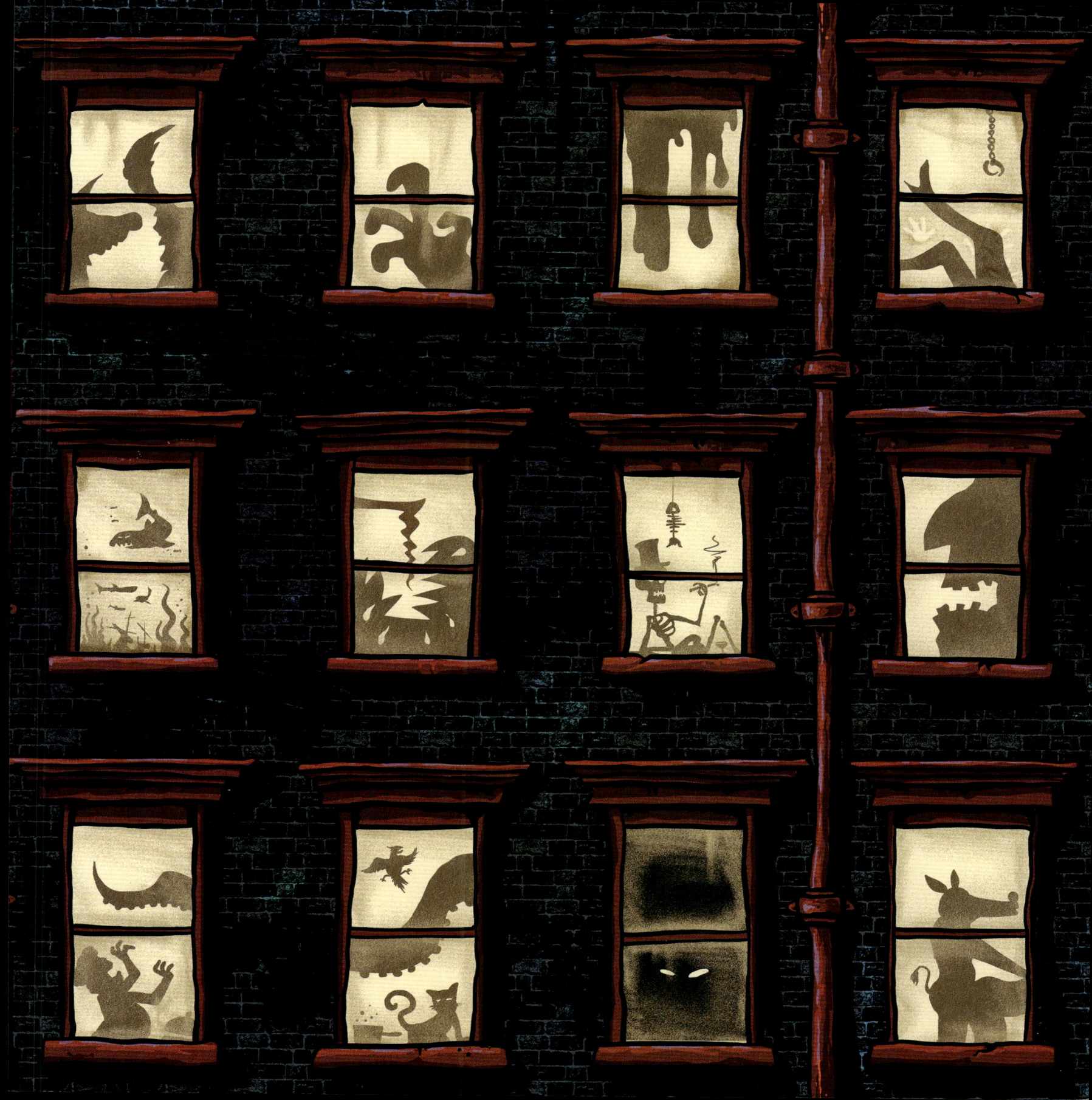

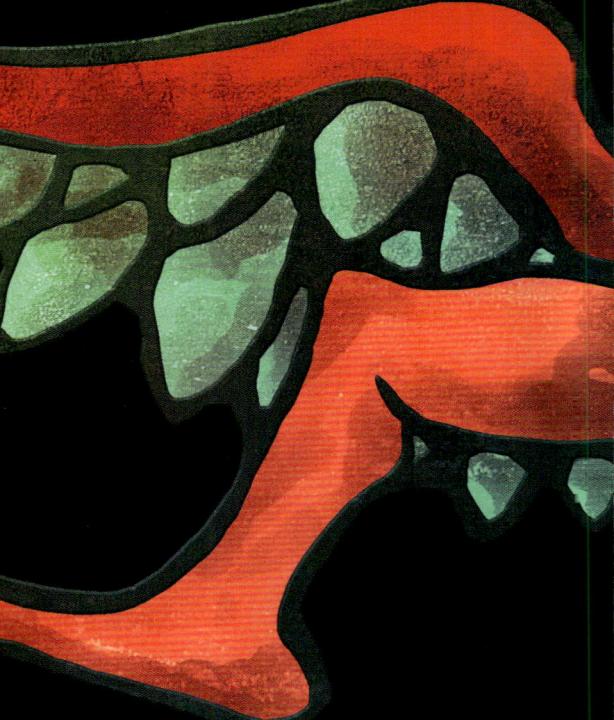

CHAPTER 14

Goodnight and Thank You

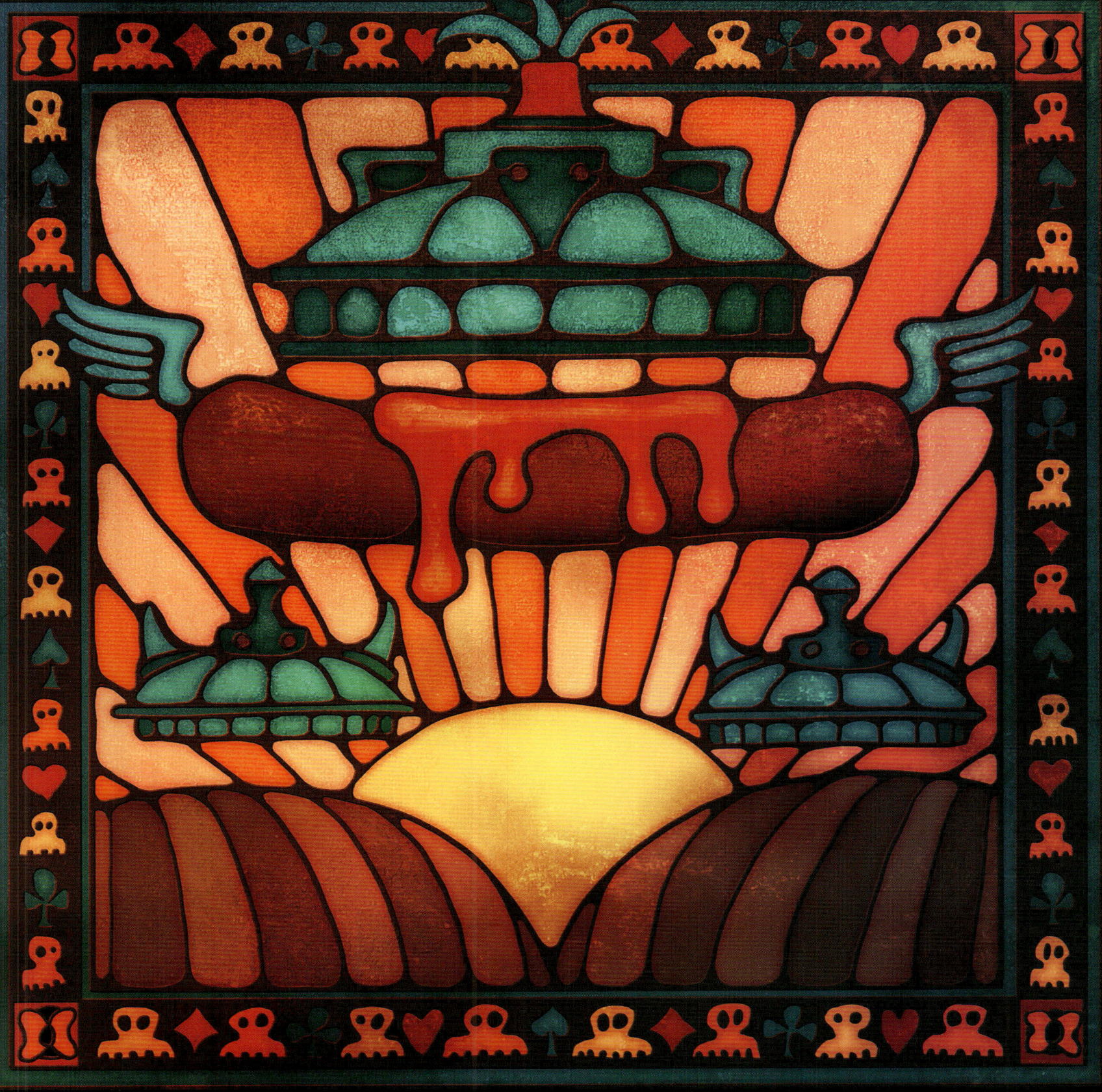

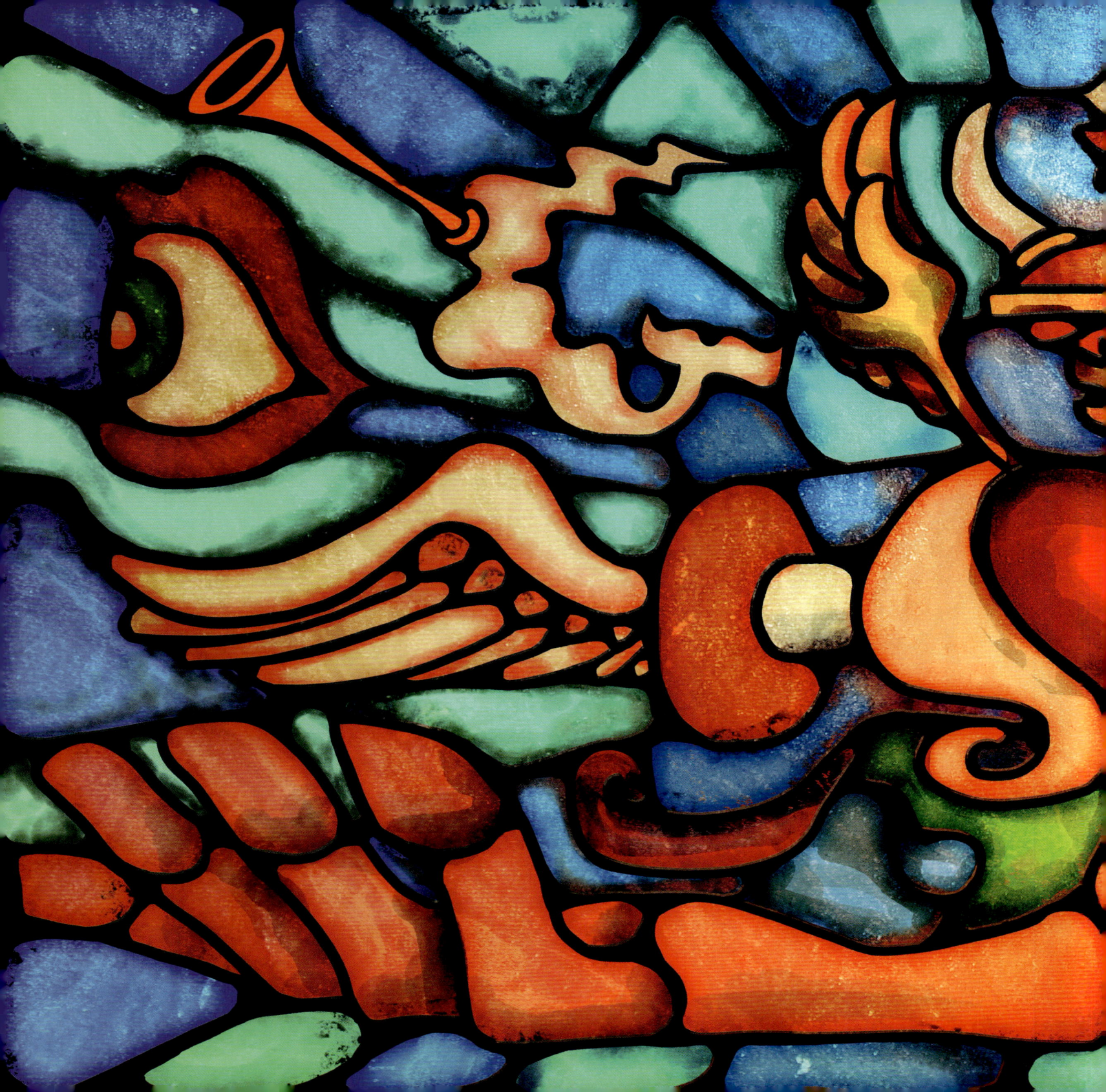

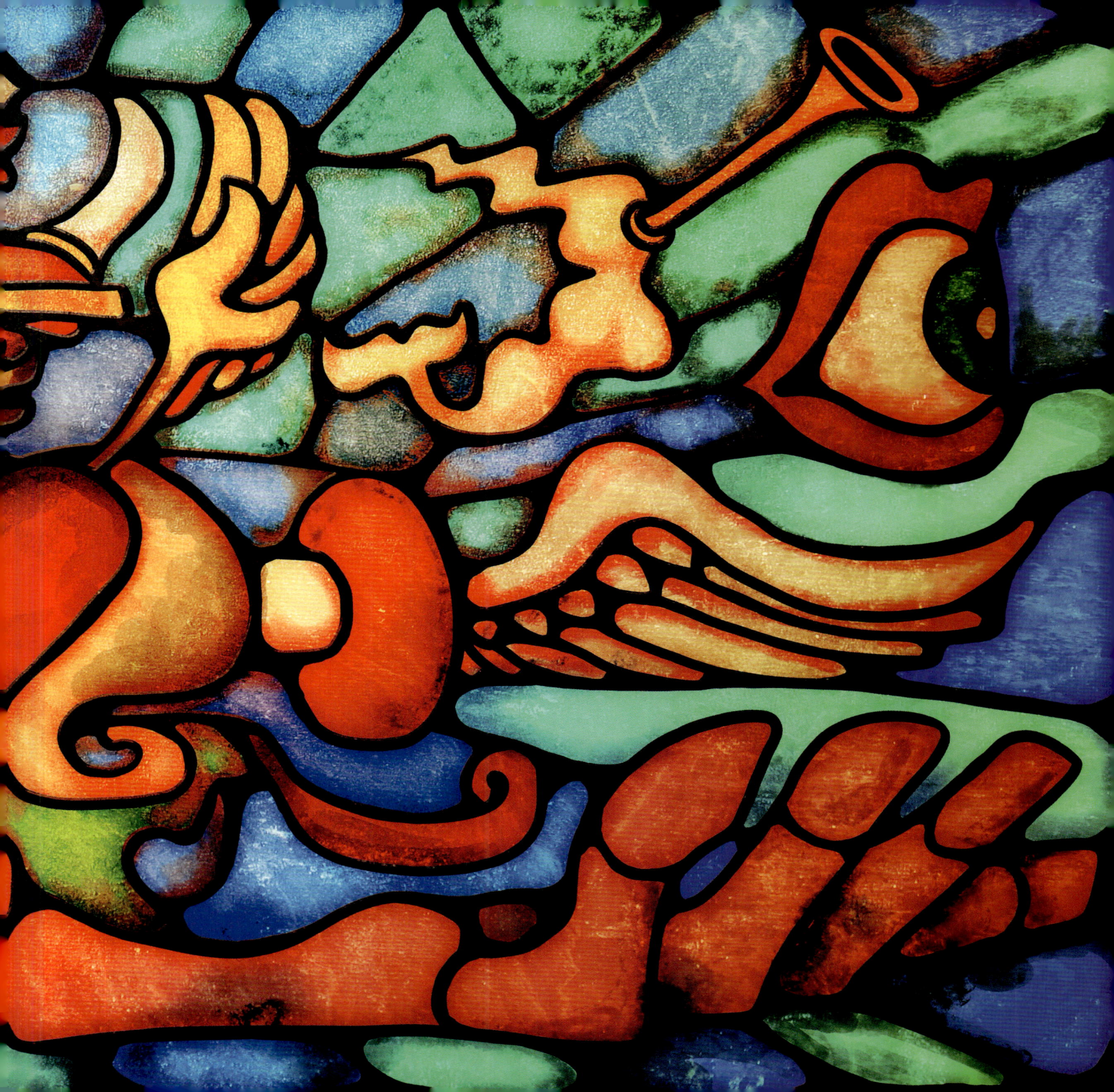

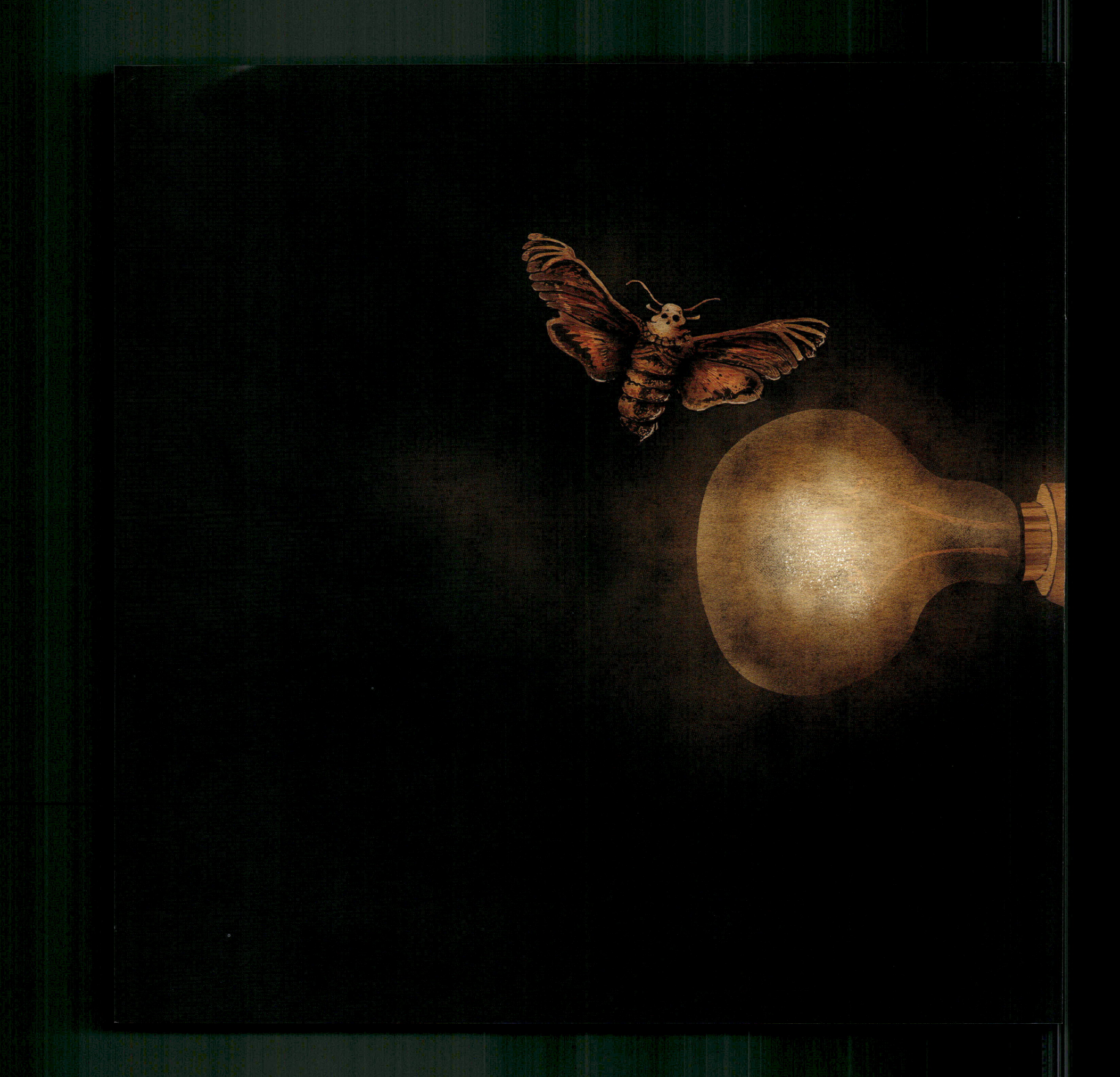

CHAPTER 15

Kaptain Karnival is Alive!

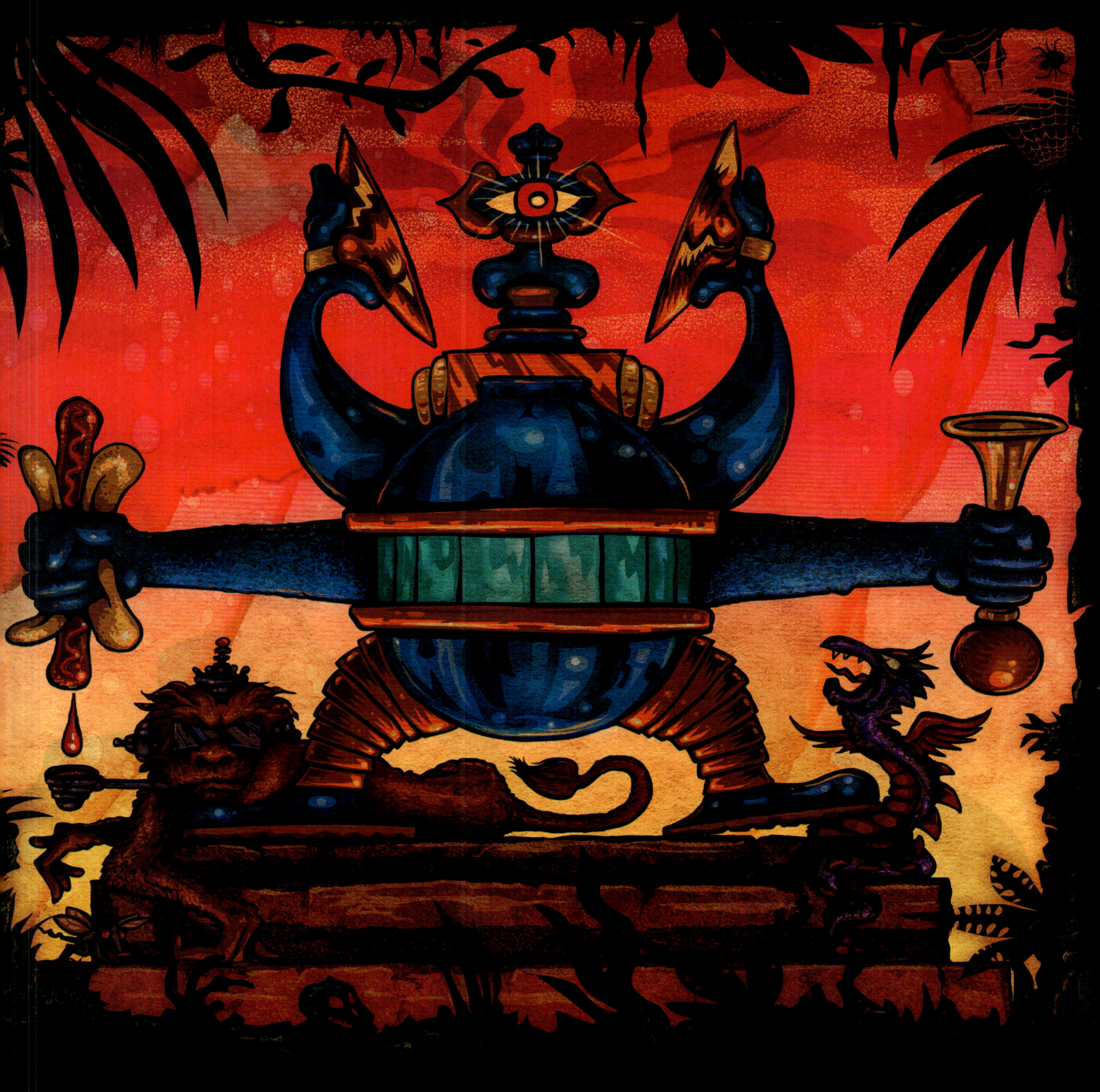

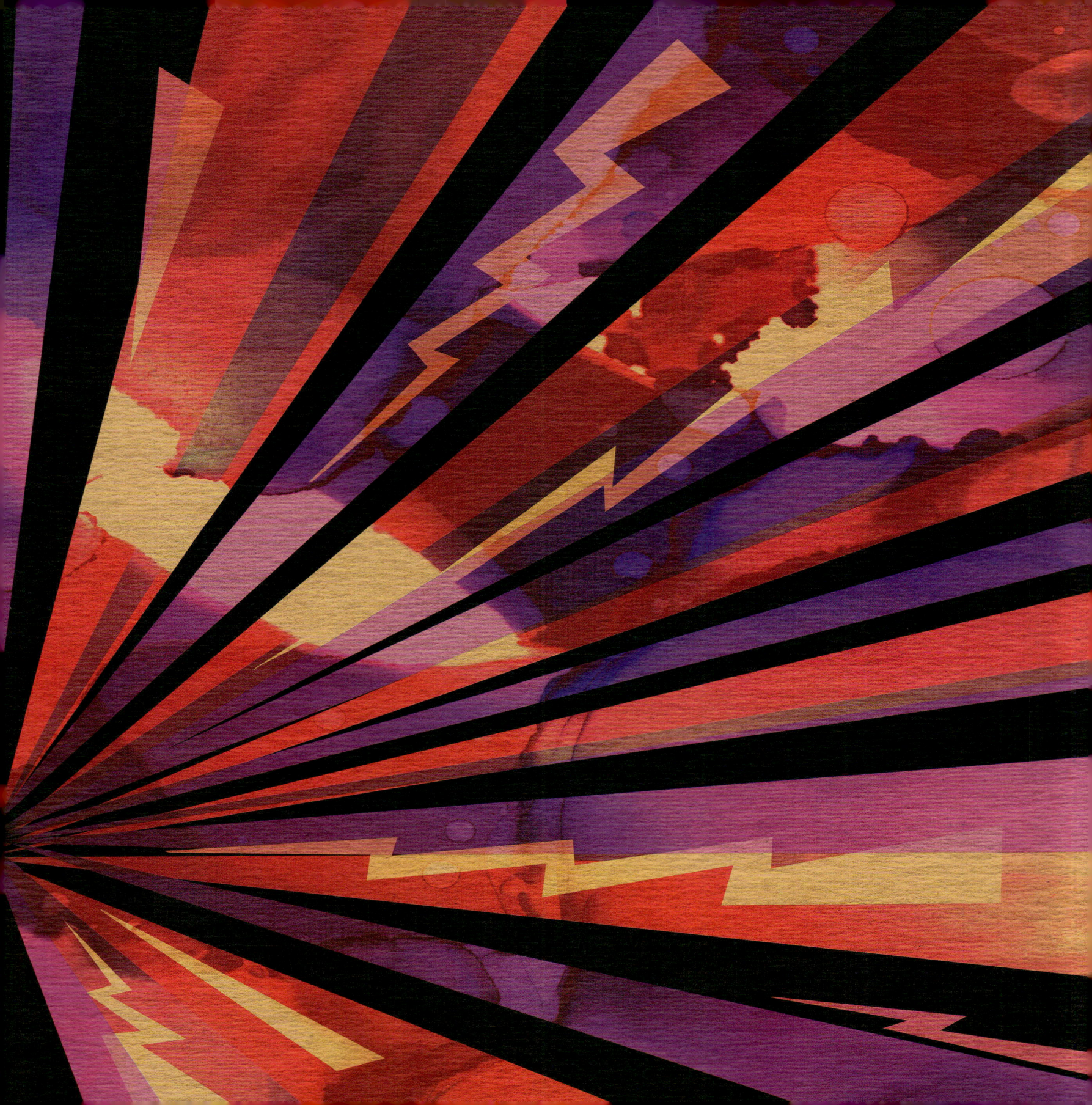

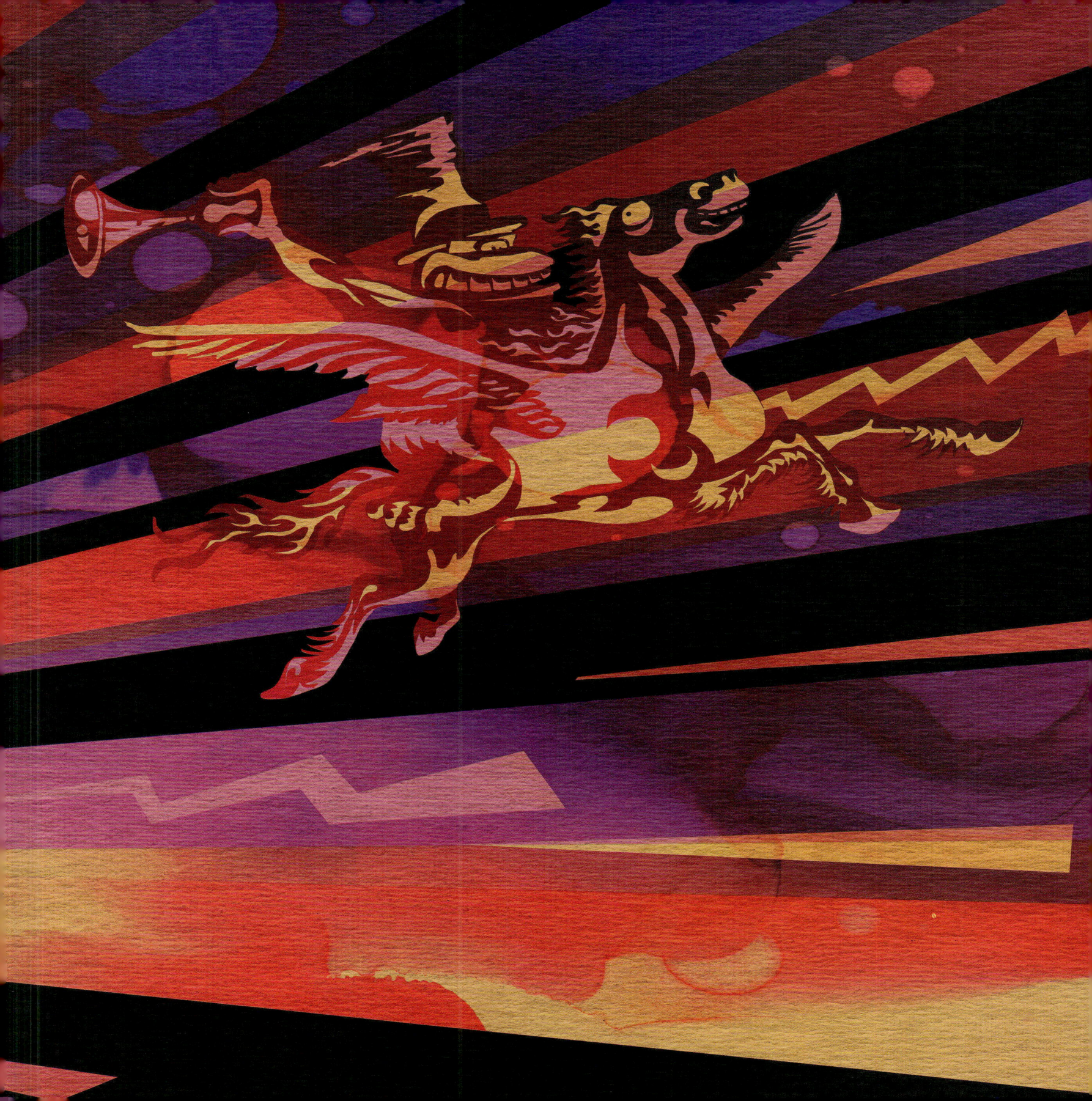

Jem Stone's
LEGEND OF KAPTAIN KARNIVAL

Music & pictures by
JEM PANUFNIK

All music written, arranged and performed by Jem Panufnik except:
Everybody's Hugging the Horse - horns arranged and performed by Dominic Glover
Voluptuoso - guitars by William Mazzarella
Rejoice and Shake Ass - guitars by Reuben Godden
The Laundrette Conspiracy - clarinet by Ben Castle, bass guitar by Sam Godden
Moose Knuckle Sandwich - horns arranged and performed by Dominic Glover, bass guitar by Sam Godden,
lead elephanti-trumpeting by Dominic Glover
Knead Us to Temptation - saxophone by Ben Castle
Late Night Check-in at the Neon Tuxedo Hotel - clarinet by Ben Castle,
trumpet by Dominic Glover, guitars by Dylan Barnes
Good Night and Thank You - guitars by Reuben Godden, bass guitar by Sam Godden
Strings by the Catgut Ensemble conducted by Hilary Spreadingham

Mixed and produced in the Funk Cabin by Jem Panufnik for Jem Stone Productions
Mastering by Doctor Moody in the Moodio, Bristol

The album can also be streamed or downloaded from most platforms if you don't have a CD player!

Jem's massive love and thanks:
Most of all to my Mischievous Marvellous Misch;
Colin at Velocity Press
Ben, Dom, Sam, Reubs, William and Dyl for their fantastic musical contributions not just here but over very many years;
Rox, Mum and my Panufnik, Giancovich and M-S clans; the unstoppable Bob Hinks;
My beloved Breaded Oyster crew & Finger Lickin' soul brothers Justin & Abel; Doc "happy" Moody
Nick Hollywood; Joe Storer; Nathan Simm; Dave Jenkins; Chris Bailey; Strictly Kev; David "hey girlfriend!" Levy; James Avon;
Lee my co-Heister, The Murphstar, Rennie Derrek Pilgrem; Dieter Steffmann; Parry and all at Everbest Printing

Moose Knuckle Sandwich is dedicated to the memory of Queen Janette Slack
who properly caned it wherever she went, yes she did, yes she did.

See more of Jem's art & music at JemPanufnik.com
Find your soulful beast at KaptainKarnival.com

1

Kaptain Karnival is Dead

2

Everybody's Hugging the Horse

3

Island of the Snake People

4

Cardiac Cadillac

5

Voluptuoso

6

Rejoice and Shake Ass

7

She Rip Spandex

8

The Laundrette Conspiracy

9

Moose Knuckle Sandwich

10

Knead Us to Temptation

11

Chili con Carnage

12

Serendipity Blues

13

Late Night Check-in at the Neon Tuxedo Hotel

14

Goodnight and Thank You

15

Kaptain Karnival is Alive!